HOW ST
FELL

HENRY KELLY

GILL AND MACMILLAN

First published in 1972
Gill and Macmillan Ltd
2 Belvedere Place
Dublin 1
and in London through association with the
Macmillan
Group of Publishing Companies

Cover designed by Cor Klaasen

SBN 7171 0632 2

Printing history:
10 9 8 7 6 5 4 3 2 1

Printed in the Republic of Ireland by
Cahill and Co. Limited
Parkgate Printing Works, Dublin 8

CONTENTS

ACKNOWLEDGEMENTS

Many more people than are aware of it helped in the writing of this book: journalists whose stories I have drawn on and whose reports proved invaluable. Others are politicians and those not directly involved in politics but whose help was perhaps even the more useful for that. I will not presume that they would want me to list their names. I have no way of knowing that they would want to be identified with the finished product.

Some of my colleagues in the *Irish Times* in Belfast and London were of great assistance: the reports from James Downey, London Editor, and his colleague Conor Brady on the evolution of the Stormont crisis from the Westminster end were invaluable. They helped me understand the principles at least of what happened and if they could go no further on details the fault was mine, not theirs.

In Belfast my colleagues Renagh Holohan, Martin Cowley, Gillian Smyth and Noreen Caffrey may not realise how much they helped by sharing my reporting duties in April when this work was written. I am grateful to them all.

Two other journalists in Belfast, Vincent Browne, Northern News Editor of the *Irish Press* and Liam Hourican, Northern Correspondent of Radio Telefís Éireann, were automatically willing to plunge into every page of this text when I asked them. They corrected mistakes and Vincent Browne particularly took time off from his own work in progress to help me. I am grateful to them both for their help.

I am indebted to an undefinable spirit in the *Irish Times* organisation at every level which makes it possible and worthwhile for one to undertake such a venture as this.

For the chapter dealing with the failure of reform in Northern Ireland I have drawn almost completely on a brilliant if small publication produced last September by a group of Northern Catholics who then, and I believe still now, prefer anonymity. Their 'Commentary on the White Paper entitled a "Record of Constructive Change"' was invaluable to me.

Finally: to my wife Marjorie who has lived through it all and survived, who has read the text, counted the words and made the tea, I am doubly grateful: for her work and her unfailing enthusiasm.

INTRODUCTION

So much has happened in the fifty years of the Northern Ireland State, particularly in the last four years and even more particularly in the last twelve months, that the temptation is to include everything, to see each incident as playing a vital part in what eventually happened less than three months ago. Alternatively there is in many circles a tendency to dismiss almost everything that happened as of no real or vital importance in the downfall of the parliament and government of Northern Ireland. Such a school of thought sees what did eventually happen as merely the acting-out of an inevitability.

The truth, and where the real significance is to be found, lies somewhere between the two. On the one hand Northern Ireland always had within its own power the potential to be a success. At the same time its overall dependence on and subservience to the British parliament meant it would always act in accordance with Westminster in economic matters at least. Its failure to adopt and stick to British principles in other fields, such as the political for example, would in the end play its part in the downfall of the fifty-year-old parliamentary system. The Northern Ireland story, the hows and whys of the fall of Stormont, begins in many places. Essentially it is the story of the last year, when a whole vast accumulation of events, policies and decisions gathered together to work against the very system they had been designed to assist. It was searching for fresh answers – and finding them temporarily – that brought Stormont down.

When the British parliament at Westminster passed the Government of Ireland Act in 1920, the 32-county country was politically divided for the first time in its life. Two states, Northern Ireland and the Irish Free State came into existence : both were born out of war and into war. Neither has had real peace since then, but the Northern state has suffered far more, lost more sons and fathers, more of its life's blood. Partition of course did not bring the phenomenon of violence to Ireland, particularly to Northern Ireland where sectarianism had ravaged the land for centuries, raising its head in each new generation with uncanny accuracy.

But partition did bring a new violence. The state of Northern Ireland was not only split from the rest of the country, it was split within itself: its mainly Protestant population favouring the 'link with Britain', its minority of Catholics wanting union with the Free State. In varying degrees these are still the divisions today: each new issue which confronts Northern Ireland is almost certain to be met with a reaction which divides its population along the old Catholic/Protestant, minority/majority lines. A wise man in Northern Ireland would do well to bear in mind as a tragic, pathetic but alas probably true general rule: if the Protestants like it the Catholics won't.

The problems then are as they have always been beneath the surface: those of reconciliation. Of reconciling not so much two religions as two views of Irish politics.

This, for example, is basically the problem which now daily confronts the Secretary of State for Northern Ireland, Mr William Whitelaw: the details may be internment, they may be Orange marches, they may be the administration of one form or another of justice. But the underlying principle is about differing views of Irish politics, the one answer that needs to be found about reconciling these views.

The first major effort even to recognise this problem was made by Lord O'Neill of the Maine when as Captain Terence O'Neill he was Prime Minister of Northern Ireland in the late sixties. O'Neill opened a line to the Dublin government by inviting the then Taoiseach Seán Lemass to Stormont. The recognition had taken a long time but at last a Unionist and a Nationalist had seen that no solution could be found to the Irish question in the context of two hostile states. The moves by O'Neill and Lemass were extremely tentative. The reaction, while generally favourable in Dublin and among the middle-class Protestants in the whole country, was fierce among working-class Protestants in the North. Whipped on by emerging politicians on the Northern scene like Ian Paisley, the leader of the Free Presbyterian Church, the working-class Protestant had placed before him not the possible advantages of greater co-operation with his fellow countrymen but the disadvantages of any formal union with the South. Such disadvantages undoubtedly existed and still do. They were magnified however when they might have been reduced in size.

In the late 1960s Northern Ireland saw the birth of a movement which was to change the whole nature and face of Irish politics. The Civil Rights Movement, which began in places like Coalisland, Dungannon and Derry, all basically Catholic strongholds, began to press for equality between Catholic and Protestant in the North. In housing, employment and in voting rights the Protestant held the advantage. Years of government by the exclusively Protestant ruling Unionist party had greatly favoured Protestants at grass roots level where a Protestant was more likely to be employed, or to get a house, than a Catholic. With a reservoir of historical bitterness at hand, the two communities faced each other on the Civil Rights issue: the Catholics were dubbed Republicans and considered to be working less for basic civil rights than for all-Ireland Nationalism. When eventually many of the requested changes were made, they turned out to be paper reforms, ephemeral changes.

The late sixties too saw the re-emergence on the scene of the illegal Irish Republican Army ready to exploit brilliantly the unrest caused by the reaction to the Civil Rights Movement: many of the Movement's marches had been attacked by militant Protestants and in purer politics old battle-lines were drawn, between supporters and opponents of a 'fair deal for Catholics' policy. Not unnaturally the divisions were basically, as so often in the past, along sectarian lines.

In August 1969, the tensions and bitterness rose dramatically to the surface in fierce sectarian rioting. In Derry the police force, the Royal Ulster Constabulary, fought a three-day battle with rioters from the Catholic Bogside on ground familiar today as 'no-go' areas for any security personnel. The flames spread to Belfast and in Protestant/Catholic rioting the minority Catholic population came off very much the worst : ten people – the majority but not all Catholic – died in fighting between Catholic and Protestant and Catholics and the police. In the end, extra British troops had to be rushed to save a holocaust and their coming on to the streets of Belfast highlighted the anomalous situation between the Stormont and Westminster governments: ultimately the Westminster parliament was sovereign, holding overall control under the Government of Ireland Act 1920. But local autonomy on internal security matters was the preserve of Stormont.

Stormont in 1969 failed to control its own state with its own resources. Some would put the beginning of the end for Stormont very firmly at the day in August 1969 when British troops entered Derry and Belfast to the cheers of Catholics who saw them as saviours from Protestant attackers. Certainly the date spelled a most serious crisis for the local parliament and government. As a result of the security crisis in 1969 efforts were made at reform in the police, in housing, in local government, in employment and in the hearts and minds of both sides. That almost all such efforts failed completely is perhaps a vital reason why there is no Stormont today.

Events over the past three years have moved at breakneck speed. Northern Ireland has got no breathing space at all, nor for that matter did Britain or the rest of Ireland, as the crisis on all fronts unfolded before the eyes of politicians and an increasing number of British troops, committed to the North as peace-keepers but eventually ending up in a full-scale war with the IRA. The IRA itself was to split in two: into an 'Official' wing claiming broadly to be socialist and military-minded only

viii

at a point when the socialist revolution would be at hand and the 'Provisional' wing making no such claims and seeking only the initial defence of Catholics and the ultimate goal of a united Irish Ireland.

In less than four years there have been more than 300 violent deaths in Northern Ireland. In 1971 alone there were 177: the list includes men, women, children, policemen, soldiers and part-time soldiers. And the war goes on: but now there is no parliament and no regional government. Just three months ago, the British government moved dramatically and decisively to impose 'direct rule' of Northern Ireland from Westminster bringing to an end just fifty years of self-government for the one and a half million population. The whole Irish political question has been opened like an oyster. Things will never be the same again. In its fifty years Northern Ireland had six Prime Ministers, and three of them have been in office in the last four years. Such is the measure of the political crisis the state has gone through to get where it is now.

Belfast
1 May 1972

1 CHICHESTER-CLARK RESIGNS

Shortly after eleven o'clock on the morning of Friday 24 March last, Edward Heath, Prime Minister of Great Britain and Northern Ireland, rose in the House of Commons at Westminster to tell MPs what many of them hoped to hear, some feared they would hear and most, in one way or another, had expected to hear for a long time. The Stormont parliament was being suspended for one year and Britain would rule Northern Ireland directly for that period by way of a Secretary of State to be advised by a commission. There would be a periodic referendum for the population of the North on whether they wished to remain within the United Kingdom or join with the Republic of Ireland.

Mr Heath's statement was brief. What his words meant was that after nearly 52 years, Unionist government in Northern Ireland was at an end. It was also the end of the entire Stormont parliamentary system, the end of an era. For few believe that Northern Ireland will ever again have a parliament of its own. What began with the passing at Westminster of the Government of Ireland Act in 1920 and was translated into life in June 1921 when the first session of the Northern Ireland parliament sat in Belfast, was at an end.

The mechanics of the direct rule operation were underway even as the British Premier spoke. So was the reaction to the move. Already committed to the retention of Stormont, of the Northern Ireland government and of all its powers, the Stormont cabinet led by the sixth Prime Minister Mr Brian Faulkner had decided to resign if its security powers were diluted in any way by the British government. And in the end, after three days of intense speculation, and talks between the two Prime Ministers Heath and Faulkner, that was just what the British had decided upon as the beginnings of an answer to the problem of Northern Ireland. Heath had told Faulkner of his decision to assume control of every matter touching upon security in the North : police, courts, prisons, even the most minor and fundamental aspects of the entire legal system. Neither Faulkner nor his cabinet would accept the proposals and, believing that they could not continue as a credible government without them, decided to resign en bloc.

The rest was a formality : Northern Ireland Ministers would stay at their desks until the new Secretary of State, Mr William Whitelaw, was officially appointed when the necessary legislation – the Northern Ireland (Temporary Provisions) Act – was ratified by the British Commons and Lords and received the Royal Assent.

Across the board in Northern Ireland the two communities reacted along almost completely traditional lines.

For the most part, the Catholic population, totally alienated from Mr Faulkner's Unionist administration, found in the dramatic initiatives that many of its most important demands had been met. Protestant opposition varied. There were those who felt little or no regret at the passing of Stormont but genuine fear that it represented in some way or another the thin end of a wedge to put Northern Ireland into an all-Ireland Republic. These people wanted, and still do, a sure guarantee that no such event would occur and, led by such men as Paisley, there is already a growing move to have the North fully integrated with the United Kingdom. Others have threatened violence: the Vanguard movement led by Craig talked in the early days after direct rule of the eventual possibility that force would be used if 'the will of the majority were overruled'. The phraseology is vague, the situation hypothetical and the support for such activity dubious. There has been talk of creating an independent British Ulster which has brought not so much rallying support as bewilderment among people who ponder on the spectacle of Northern

2

Ireland people fighting England to keep the British way of life.

But direct rule has moved into the way of life of the people with surprising ease. It has become a fact of life. It has been accepted. Only its forms, its mechanics and its life-span cause controversy in both camps. And what led to it causes debate and discussion into the long hours.

There are those who can argue persuasively that from the day it was founded Stormont was doomed. Their logic is that of the man who accepts the inevitability of mortality among humans. But it hardly helps a consideration of how Stormont died. The parliament and state of Northern Ireland survived sectarian rioting in the twenties, thirties, and most notably the sixties. But it was in the violence of the late sixties, a violence born not intrinsically out of religious argument but out of the struggle for basic civil rights, that the seeds were first sown for a revolution which was to bring an end to the system. The final death of Stormont is the story of a year; but it is the story of a year in which death and bloodshed, hate and fear, action and reaction came together, not mysteriously, but as a result of pressures and counter-pressures, rumblings and discontents of the previous three years. If Stormont had a cancer from birth it died of a 'flu in the end.

That end was the year spanning two marches when politics and violence moved in Northern Ireland with the speed of a fictional best-seller. The road to the finale had been paved with 'ifs' and 'buts': if the Unionist party had been clever enough to support Lord O'Neill, when as Captain Terence O'Neill he had tried to be a reforming Prime Minister in the middle and late sixties, they might still have their parliament. If the Stormont and Westminster governments had not turned, in the tragic month of August 1971, to the disastrous policy of internment, then there might still be a parliament in Belfast. If . . . If . . . In the end it was Brian Faulkner who presided over the final days of Unionist rule last March, but the story begins one year earlier with the resignation of James Chichester-Clark, now Lord Moyola, as Prime Minister.

3

The fate of Chichester-Clark was that as Prime Minister for a year and a half he never really got out of the wood. From the day he took office people were wondering how long he would last, when he would fall or be pushed. As Prime Minister he was unique among Unionist leaders in that he inherited the odium which had attached to his predecessor O'Neill. As Prime Minister he presided over the disbanding of the Ulster Special Constabulary, the introduction of British troops into Northern Ireland on a vast scale, the coming of changes like the Ombudsman, the Ministry of Community Relations, the Central Housing Executive and the general and perceptible whittling away of Unionist power and monopoly at grass-roots and even central level. Try as he might through his stay as Premier he never lived down the death of the Specials. Nor for that matter did his cabinet. The B men were the heroes of the Ulster Protestant at many levels. In the cities they were the known and trusted local 'lads.' The same held true in rural areas, especially in the IRA border campaigns of the fifties and sixties. As well, Specials earned money, were given a status, a uniform, weapons, all the trappings of men whose job was valuable to the maintenance of the state. They were in every sense the defenders. When they were disbanded as part of the Hunt Report proposals in 1969 the effect was dramatic and traumatic.

Apart from the rioting which followed the news, in which loyalist mobs in the Shankill Road in Belfast killed an unarmed RUC man and later had three local men shot dead by British troops, the men who had been Specials were humiliated in the eyes of both communities. Their disbandment cast doubts on their integrity, their ability and their performance. They were stood down and they felt let down. They were demobbed but they may as well have been discharged in disgrace. And right through his period in office this was to be thrown in Chichester-Clark's face. If Ian Paisley did it every time he made a speech, it rang true in the minds of Protestants in every area of Northern Ireland. 'Bring Back the B Men' would grace walls alongside 'Chi-Chi Must Go'. But the B men, the reforms, the

4

security situation, these pressures were in the end only contributory factors in the eventual downfall of Chichester-Clark.

A more significant and vital factor in his demise was the single great issue which had its roots in August 1969: the existence of areas in Belfast, Derry and other towns in the North where the police did not operate and where the British Army went warily, if at all. The 'no-go' areas as they were called were the real death of Chichester-Clark and in them is bound the whole security dilemma which re-emerged to face the British government, then a Labour administration, from 15 August 1969 onwards. If he had the end of the B men thrown in his face for a year and a half, Chichester-Clark was equally tormented by the 'no-go' areas during his entire period in office. In the end they hastened his resignation.

When the Scarman Tribunal report was published in April this year it clearly stated that in August 1969 when ten people were killed in sectarian rioting in several centres in the North and when thousands of Catholics were made homeless after Protestant attacks, there was neither an IRA plot to bring down the state of Northern Ireland nor a Protestant pogrom against Catholics. It wasn't within the terms of reference of the tribunal, under Mr Justice Leslie Scarman, to say what had been the effects of August 1969. Had it been, the conclusion that after the rioting in Belfast and particularly in Derry the Royal Ulster Constabulary was finished as a force capable of patrolling Catholic areas would have been inescapable.

In Northern Ireland the fact that appearances are more important than reality is a running tragedy. The state lives, and Scarman did point this out, on 'ghosts'. And it lives on myths that don't need to have originated in 1690 or 1916. A day is generally long enough. And the 'fact' taken by Catholics in Belfast after August was that the RUC had been in league with Protestants to wipe them out. The result was that even towards the end of the month when British troops were still being treated as saviours in Catholic ghettoes, those ghettoes were barricaded and closed to the officers of the law. Whether this was justifiable or not is not at issue : enough has been written about the murders committed by some policemen who have never been found or charged to explain Catholic fears. What is important is that after August policing in Catholic areas was finished.

In April 1970 Paisley and his Protestant Unionist colleague William Beattie won two by-elections in Bann Side and South Antrim almost exclusively on the security situation and later John Laird held his father's official Unionist seat in St Anne's, Belfast, not by supporting government policy, but by attacking the law and order measures which Chichester-Clark was carrying out. Week after week during his term of office Unionist associations, Unionist groups and committees, and Unionist opinion generally were hitting at the Prime Minister because of the no-go areas. Isolated incidents – men whose cars were stolen and who later paid ransoms to get them back from places like the Catholic Ballymurphy estate – were daily peddled in the political market-place as evidence to support the theory that because such areas existed there was a total breakdown of law and order and government policies were ruining the state. The most familiar words, for example, in the most familiar Stormont debates during Chichester-Clark's reign were 'law and order'. The debates were not of course really debates: from the Opposition came the reasonable and true case that the Catholic community did not trust the security forces under Stormont's power and wouldn't let their guard down for a moment. From the right-wing of the Unionist party came the hankering after the B men and the broadsides on the government. In the middle were the Prime Minister and his Home Affairs minister, Robert Porter, literally trying to make the ends, of satisfying Protestants and ensuring law and order throughout the North, meet.

Chichester-Clark weathered many storms surprisingly well. When elected he was generally reckoned a temporary leader for the Unionist party. When O'Neill was pushed the Parliamentary party, by one vote, went for

Chichester-Clark instead of Faulkner on the grounds that the winner was a 'decent man you could trust rather than a clever one you couldn't'. It was certainly the hall-mark of his career that the huge, ambling ex-Irish Guard always looked as if he wished he were at home feeding cattle or riding to hounds. He had at least looked honest and tried generally to act so. If he failed it was through a mixture of incompetence and lack of understanding as much as any bloody-minded desire to hang on to Unionist power. In another country at another time he would be the last person even to want to enter politics, never mind become the senior executive. In early 1969 there had been less than 3,000 British troops in the North. By the time he resigned the figure was 10,000 and rising. When he took office Belfast was an open, walkable city. When he left a corrugated 'peace-line' dividing Catholic and Protestant areas ran through it to testify to Unionism's failure. On the credit side more reforming laws found their way on to the statute books in a year than would have been dreamed of by any Unionist before him. He may be said to have at least put into black and white what were only ideas in Terence O'Neill's head. As he left office it was a certainty that somewhere in a drawer marked 'Honours' in Whitehall there was a title waiting for him.

It would be wrong, though not totally, to see in his resignation the final beginning of the end for Stormont. It was not that he was the second-last chance, no question of après him the deluge. It was more a question of how he went that was important. Nothing in his career was quite as vital to the end of Stormont as the manner of his going. His term of office was studded with security problems and of these clearly the lack of policing in Catholic areas was the major cause of tension. There is no evidence to support the thesis, admittedly not advanced with any great enthusiasm anywhere, that Chichester-Clark was interested in restoring peace and law and order to every area simply in order to remain in power. Unlike his cabinet colleague and successor, Mr Faulkner, he was never really much taken with the job in the first place. He wanted law and order restored because he was convinced it was a good thing – nothing more, nothing less. And when finally he got embroiled in a struggle with Westminster over the way to achieve this he didn't resign in a fit of pique but because he, and others, believed there was no other way to tell Westminster what was happening. By the time he was due to go in March last year there was not yet at Westminster the type of concerned interest in Northern Ireland that there should have been if politicians there had been conscious of the logic of the British Army's intervention back in 1969.

Nothing, it appears, had driven home the message to the British government that sooner, rather than later, they would have to do something about Northern Ireland. At the height of the August troubles in 1969 Harold Wilson and James Callaghan, Prime Minister and Home Secretary, had certainly seen the need for swift action. But their political sight went no further. An opportunity was certainly lost then. And lives would be lost before that chance arose once more. Events under Chichester-Clark had a snowballing effect on the whole situation: each new twist not only constituted a crisis in itself but added to the over-all deteriorating situation. But it was Chichester-Clark's relationship with the British government that is most vital in this investigation into the end of Stormont. For that relationship constituted a re-awakening in the British government of the need for action only when it was at an end: in other words Chichester-Clark had to resign to make Westminster pay any real attention. And as soon as he did, unfortunately for the long-term future of Northern Ireland, the man who took over was dedicated to quick results, positive achievements and visible signs of victory. And in Northern Ireland you just cannot have those things, no matter what side of the fence you are on.

What happened between Chichester-Clark and the British government was this. All along he had tried to do his best to co-operate with the Labour government on every issue from major reforms to day-to-day and more routine affairs. But as the pressure mounted on him within his own party because of the security situation he felt it fair that he should ask Westminster to play its part too. Under Wilson and Callaghan and the Labour government this had not been so much of an issue. The Conservatives came to power at a crucial point, particularly for Chichester-Clark. There had been, in the first months of 1970, pretty fierce riots in Ballymurphy, a Catholic area in the Upper Springfield Road area of Belfast. In March the government won a vote of confidence in the Commons at Stormont for its security policies, but it lost five back-benchers who either abstained or voted against the motion and were expelled from the Unionist Parliamentary party. The Labour government, still regarding Northern Ireland in the same light as it had in the previous August, remained committed to a policy that would not offend or appear to attack the Catholic population in any way. The 'long haul' policy, although it would only be called that much later, was the order of the day.

By June, with the Tories in power, things were different. In Catholic eyes, the first week of July 'proved' there was a change of policy when British troops curfewed and searched the Catholic lower Falls Road area, a rabbit-warren of tiny streets and houses. Three people were killed, rioting lasted hours and the curfew itself two days. It was the type of operation the Unionists had been de-manding but it probably did not reflect a change in policy so much as drastic underestimation by the then General Officer Commanding troops in the North, Sir Ian Freeland. He ordered the operation and, at a time when tempers might have cooled after the first arms searches, lost his head and went for military successes. Despite a large arms haul, these were massively outweighed in terms of lost Catholic sympathy for the Army.

If there had been at the start of July the slightest hope that the 'no go' areas would be brought to an end by tough military moves, the Falls curfew finished that idea. Just as the police had lost the confidence of Catholics after August 1969, so the British Army lost their con-fidence when they were seen, as far as the Catholics were

9

concerned, to be supporting on the ground the Stormont government and system. Tough measures had been asked for by the Unionists and, to the Catholic's way of thinking, they had been given. Distrust of the Conservatives had been translated into a very harsh reality: the Army was no better than the B men or the RUC. For the rest of the year the smouldering hatred of the Army would continue in Catholic hearts and minds. By the end of 1970 even high-ranking Army officers like Major-General Tony Farrar-Hockley, Commander of Land Forces, were openly confident that the security crisis was past the worst and that things were on the mend. But in the 'no-go' areas the trouble was only starting. As the Stormont government warned aloud that the illegal Irish Republican Army would build its organisation behind the barricades, the real tragedy of the 'no-go' areas was working away day by day. And that tragedy was not that any branch of the IRA used the freedom of the barricaded areas to recruit or train, but that the reformed, unarmed civilianised RUC was never given a chance to operate in Catholic areas. In other words, the working-class Catholic population of Belfast never saw the effects of what was meant to be a major change in the system: a new-look police force.

As 1971 dawned the trouble began again and despite Army attempts to talk to the now openly-operating Provisional IRA the first British soldier was killed in early February. More trouble would follow but at this point Chichester-Clark really began to search for a way of explaining to the British government just what was happening and what would happen if the situation continued. At this point there seems little doubt that the Major himself thought military tactics were the ones to pursue. When the enemy can be seen you go after him and get him. It seems not to have been a priority to try and win the minds of the ghettoes, just to put policemen back into them. The British Home Secretary, Mr Reginald Maudling, who can justly claim to know as little about Northern Ireland as any other British politician before him or since, was allowed to get on with his job by Heath. That job, as far as the people in Northern Ireland were concerned, was at best undramatic and at worst downright non-existent. In early March he came to Belfast and quite pretentiously arranged to address MPs and Senators in the Main Hall of Stormont. The meeting was a ham-fisted fiasco. Opposition MPs turned up and Austin Currie, SDLP MP for East Tyrone, said afterwards: 'If that is all he came to tell us I'd have been better off at home watching Romper Room.' The feeling was shared from Chichester-Clark down. As John Hume, SDLP MP for Foyle, said, the visit had raised hopes that some British initiative was on the way but the speech had done nothing to satisfy those hopes.

Whatever was going to come from the British it would not come from Mr Maudling. At the time it was rumoured that he had come to tell the Unionists that they could not have any more of the things they wanted; no more troops, no more curfews, no more search and swoop operations, and very certainly and firmly no internment of IRA suspects without trial. Looking back now one wonders about Mr Maudling's interest in and awareness of the problems. He seems to have underestimated the situation grossly, and he was guiding his British cabinet colleagues at the time. There was still plenty of time as far as Maudling was concerned.

But as Chichester-Clark saw things, the impending crisis was now only weeks, rather than months away. As sporadic rioting went on he tried again and again to impress on the British government what was happening: his authority was flaunted in incident after incident. IRA funerals, with volleys of shots over graves and marching lines of black-bereted men, were held in Belfast. In the second week of March three young off-duty Scottish soldiers were found shot dead through the head on a lonely country lane just north of Belfast city. The enormity and coldbloodedness of the triple murder still lingers in Belfast and throughout the North. The deaths were a crushing blow to the Prime Minister's dwindling confidence; just the sort of incident to make him feel his government had lost

11

control completely of the security situation. The murders were no worse than what could have been done at any time by three bullets in any of the many shooting incidents in Belfast or Derry.

But they made up the Prime Minister's mind : he would try once again to warn the British government of what was around the corner and if that failed he would resign. On Tuesday 16 March he flew to London for a surprise visit to 10 Downing Street. There he had talks with Mr Maudling, with the Prime Minister, Mr Heath, and with the British Defence Secretary Lord Carrington. He asked for more troops, not for repressive measures against Catholics, not to save his own political skin about which he cared very little, but because he could see no other way to end no-go areas. His view was that there would have to be quick military response to violence, a return to, at first, Army patrolling and eventually to joint Army–RUC patrols. Some day, he hoped, the RUC would then be able to go it alone in Catholic areas. He told the English ministers that if they would not agree to these suggestions he would resign. They didn't believe him. He was to them the sort of officer and gentleman to whom one would impart the need for remaining in office and, like the first man over the hill, he would agree and stay on. He had other ideas. The can had become impossible to carry. On Thursday afternoon he told the Commons that he had got just over a thousand extra troops, and that they would be arriving immediately. His statement–did its best to dress up the failure of his London trip.

On Friday afternoon there was a Cabinet meeting at Stormont Castle at which every member of the Cabinet impressed upon Chichester-Clark the need to stay in office. There was no-one, his colleagues promised him, who could take over with any confidence. Brian Faulkner, who had stood by the Prime Minister for the previous 18 months, was not particularly verbose on this aspect of the situation but he did basically seem to want Chichester-Clark to stay at this stage. He still retained the view, of course, that if he were Prime Minister himself there would be no problems at all. Late on Friday it was announced that Carrington and some officials would fly into Belfast the next day for more talks. On the Saturday morning a silent Carrington flew in, met the cabinet, talked and listened and left equally taciturn. The Prime Minister resigned later that night. His resignation statement was careful and summed up the ideas behind his weeks and months of coaxing and arguing with the British. He pointed to the recurring anomaly between power and responsibility brought about by the relationship between Westminster and Stormont. The statement was in effect, though Chichester-Clark cannot have intended it to be so, a confession from a Unionist Prime Minister that Unionism had failed and that there was only one course open to the British: direct rule. Chichester-Clark said in his final statement: 'I have decided to resign because I can see no other way of bringing home to all concerned the realities of the present constitutional, political and security situation.

'On Thursday I indicated to parliament the result of my discussions earlier in the week with British Ministers. I welcomed then as I do now the response of the United Kingdom government, particularly in the matter of troop reinforcements. The situation however is simply this: it is apparent that public and parliamentary opinion in Northern Ireland looks to the Northern Ireland government for measures which can bring the current IRA campaign swiftly to an end. I have expressed to British Ministers the full force of this opinion and have pressed upon them my view that some further initiative is required. While they have agreed to take any feasible steps open to them to intensify the effort against the IRA, it remains the professional military view – and one which I indeed have often expressed myself – that it would be misleading the Northern Ireland community to suggest that we are faced with anything but a long haul, and that such initiatives as can be taken are unlikely to effect a radical improvement in the short term. The Northern Ireland population must therefore continue to exercise the greatest patience and

13

restraint, without which no efforts made by the security forces can succeed. I remain convinced that the policies we have been following whether in the social, economic or security fields have been realistic, and if fully understood would offer the best hope of bringing Northern Ireland out of its present difficulties. I am resigning forthwith as leader of the Unionist party and have asked the Chief Whip to make arrangements for the election of a new leader.'

So he went. As he departed the election lights shone brightly for Faulkner who had the support of the entire cabinet when the chips were down. But Chichester-Clark had to resign for his own sake and to explain his policies. He must be the only person who had to resign in politics to make people understand what he had meant while in office. The British government obviously did not believe he would go. When he did they momentarily panicked. And that panic lasted long enough to see Brian Faulkner through the first few months. But it seems probable that Edward Heath at least had begun to read more into Chichester-Clark's resignation than most and had decided that Stormont could have just one more chance, one more year to try and make Unionist control work. After that there would be complete take-over.

The importance of the British intervention in those dramatic days in August 1969 cannot be overlooked in this whole context since it gave rise to the very circumstances which Chichester-Clark tried to indicate in his resignation statement. The British Labour government in August 1969 did not really carry through the logic of its own policy : if the Government of Ireland Act allowed the British government control over the armed forces and if the use of those forces came to be the only thing of political import in Northern Ireland then the situation could be changed in one of two ways.

Either, unthinkably, the British could give the Unionists a free hand in controlling the Army, or they could take away security powers completely. As the Army became more and more embroiled in Northern Ireland, as soldiers

14

began to die and the civilian casualty list mounted alongside the rate of explosions and 'general incidents' this
second – indeed only – choice would emerge clearly. It
was there in 1969 but it was recognised by only a few.
Certainly there was a tenable point of view to balance it :
to have taken over in 1969 might have made things worse.
It is easy to say now that this couldn't possibly have been
the case, but those were emotionally-charged days and
instant cures rather than long-term solutions were the
order of the moment. But when British troops walked into
Belfast and Derry in 1969 it was a tragedy and an expen-
sive one that a Secretary of State didn't walk in after them.
The Unionist mind is for ever returning to those days and
speaking of how the Prime Minister gave away Stormont's
powers and sold out their security forces. The truth of the
matter is that it was not the famous Downing Street meeting which brought about the involvement of the British
Army on a wide scale but the involvement of the British
Army which brought about the meeting. When Harold
Wilson decided that the North's own security forces should
be 'called out to a man' before troops went in he had
provided the basis of proof that in August 1969 Northern
Ireland couldn't have gone it alone. Every resource available to the government of the day was stretched to the
limit and yet that situation was still deteriorating.

And as has been pointed out there was hardly a voice
raised in August 1969 when the Army did arrive. If politicians, commentators, ordinary people are honest they
will admit that the introduction of troops was vitally
necessary at that point if a full-scale civil and religious
war was not to erupt. Once the Army was in, then, the
questions raised by the outgoing Chichester-Clark became
the vital ones but they were not tackled until the situation
had gone out of control. The Thursday before he resigned,
Chichester-Clark had used some prophetic words in the
Commons at Stormont. He accepted that there had been
much speculation about his continuing in office. 'There
has been a good deal of speculation in recent days', he
told MPs, 'about changes in personalities. However per-

sonalities may change, these facts of which I have spoken will not change. Anyone who comes to this Dispatch Box will have to face them just as I have done. And I ask the House to remember too that we do no service to Northern Ireland if we snuff out the present campaign in ways which merely make a resumption at some other time and with increased popular support, inevitable. Our aim is not just to defeat the present vicious conspiracy but to create conditions in which such men and such activities can never prosper again.' By 'snuff out' he meant internment. In two short speeches here, and in his resignation statement, Chichester-Clark had shown more insight into the problems than in all his previous statements put together.

As he ambled along the Stormont corridors the logic of the British military presence and its inherent political involvement had dawned on him. The smallness of Northern Ireland, the pettiness of its parliament, the futility of its politics, all were very much reduced in size when the state was unable to control itself. You do not ask a man to protect you and not expect at some time that he will want to say how that protection shall be carried out. This was what happened in Northern Ireland eventually and this was what began under the premiership of James Chichester-Clark. There were no quick solutions, no instant answers, no visible ways of getting any Unionist government off the security hook. It was to be the fate of Stormont, however, that at the moment when it could possibly have learned from the mistakes of its recent past, just when it might have scraped a 'pass' in the exam for effort to bring the two communities together by a show of magnanimity from Unionism and a genuine desire to share the spoils of power, it would be entrusted to a man very impressed with his own ability, and one who had supreme confidence in that ability to solve all problems. That man was Brian Faulkner and if he heard the words of his former Prime Minister that Thursday in Stormont he chose to ignore them as he took up office.

2 FAULKNER TAKES OVER

The morning of Tuesday, 23 March 1971 saw the huge and impressive Great Hall at Stormont packed with journalists from all over the world. As time ticked away and reporters waited for the Unionist party Chief Whip Mr John Dobson to announce the name of the new party leader no-one had the slightest doubt about the result: Brian Faulkner had been voted into office by an overwhelming majority of his parliamentary colleagues and would be Prime Minister within hours. The days since Chichester-Clark's resignation had been full, if not quite packed, with rumour and speculation about whether there would even be a contest for the vacancy. Faulkner had the job sewn up while his predecessor was only rising from his seat and the late candidature of William Craig, who never had the slightest chance of winning in any event, did nothing to upset the foregone conclusion of the result.

When Dobson appeared at the top of a forbidding flight of steps he had the voting in his hand on a small scrap of paper. His walk to the table at the foot of the stairs was slow and shaking – he was at the time in poor health – and he announced the result quietly and with little emotion. As he did, Craig appeared on a balcony overlooking the hall. There was as yet no sign of Faulkner. Dobson told reporters: 'The voting for leadership of the Unionist party was as follows: Mr William Craig 4 votes, Mr Brian Faulkner 26 votes. Accordingly I declare Mr Faulkner duly elected as leader of the Unionist Parliamentary party.' He added that neither candidate had voted in the election.

A few seconds later Brian Faulkner appeared and fairly skipped down the steps to speak to the press. Dapper, neat, looking every inch a confident politician, he began his statement with an air of a headmaster who has come to address the boys on an important topic over which he has full control although he realises it has them very worried. As the flash-bulbs blinked he spoke: 'My most important single aim is to restore confidence throughout the whole community. Without that all else would be futile. Obviously the kernel of our immediate problems is the law and order situation. Let me say right away that I am convinced that what we need on this front are not new principles but practical results on the ground in the elimination not only of terrorism and sabotage, but of riots and disorder. The basic principle must clearly be that the rule of law shall operate in all parts of Northern Ireland, so that the security that goes with the rule of law can be enjoyed by all our citizens.

'It is the responsibility of the police and army to put that principle into effect. My administration will give them every support. I will not expect harsh measures or repressive measures – no law-abiding citizen will have anything whatsoever to fear from my administration – but I will be looking for efficient measures. When the governments at Westminster and at Stormont take decisions on these matters we will certainly insist not only on effective action by the security forces but – and this is equally important – swift and decisive reaction to any trouble which might occur'.

The Faulkner style was set in those first few lines of his first public statement as Prime Minister. If he felt at the time there was anything else wrong in Northern Ireland apart from security problems he didn't mention it. Right through that first short statement security seemed to be the only thing in his mind. This wasn't a hard-line right-wing attitude necessarily: it was just that Faulkner saw what had happened under Chichester-Clark and was determined that it should not continue under him. He was giving the impression of firmness. And the best way he could do it was to talk battle against the security problem. He went on to talk about the need to improve co-ordination between the RUC and the Army, of his determination that the police should not be used as a political shuttlecock and of the need which he believed most vital : that of bringing law-breakers and criminals to book. He emphasised that the programme for progress on which the previous administration had embarked would be 'energetically continued'.

Then he went on : 'In accepting the job of Prime Minister of Northern Ireland I do so because I am convinced that progress here, in all fields, depends on the maintenance of our parliament at Stormont. From it we have in the past derived great benefits both social and economic – benefits which have been enjoyed by all the people of Northern Ireland. The parliament and government of Northern Ireland must be maintained. Direct Rule would undoubtedly be an utter disaster'. So there was the second half of the policy which the new Prime Minister would follow.

One part would be to do battle with the security crisis, the other to see to it that the Unionist-dominated parliament and government would be maintained. At any or all costs. And there was even a hint at the end of his statement that he was less than fully confident in the total involvement of the British : 'We are profoundly grateful', he said as he finished, 'for all the help we have received from the United Kingdom government but I think that all would agree that our problems can only be satisfactorily solved by Ulster's own people. As an Ulsterman I can only promise to do my best for this province and I appeal to all my countrymen to help me'. That was his hand-out statement and after that he answered a few questions before going to Hillsborough to take up office officially from the Governor. As he did so, William Craig was saying that he would give the new Prime Minister a period in which to prove himself and early soundings from the Social, Democratic and Labour party led by Gerry Fitt MP seemed to suggest much the same policy would be followed there too. Craig and Fitt were looking to Faulkner to prove himself in different ways of course. That would soon be part of the trouble.

On Thursday 25th, Faulkner announced his first cabinet. Its main point was that it included Mr Harry West, a former Minister for Agriculture who had been sacked by Terence O'Neill some years previously. But there was more to West than that.

Within the Unionist party at every level, no-one apart from Craig had been such a consistent opponent of every single reform brought in in August 1969. From the high emotional point of the disbanding of the B Specials down to the reshaping of Local Government West had hammered away for a year and a half in the political company of Paisley, Craig and others at the Chichester-Clark government. Most interestingly he had, as a rural MP, attacked the plans to reform local government which were in essence an effort to take away from Unionist-controlled local authorities the 'temptations' to continue on as Lord Cameron and his committee had observed was the method of operation. Cameron had reported in 1969 on the allegations of discrimination and at local level had found many of them proved. West had even gone to the trouble of forming the West Ulster Unionist Council to which were affiliated Unionist constituency associations west of the Bann and even some Belfast associations too, who opposed change anywhere and everywhere. This council had produced a small pamphlet attacking local government reform. Mr West's name was put to it. It was called 'Faulkner's Fiddle'. Mr West was now back as a Cabinet Minister. But Mr Craig was nowhere to be seen and whether it was intentional or not, the right-wing line up had been smashed in a quick blow by Faulkner: West was separated from Craig; if the West Ulster Unionist Council was to continue either it would now support Faulkner or it would do without its President, Harry West.

When asked why he had taken a Cabinet seat, West told reporters that it was time to let what had been done be accepted. 'Certain decisions were taken in the past with which I did not agree,' he said. 'But we must look to the future. I have had assurances from the Prime Minister that I can tell you about and certain others that I cannot tell you about. But I am satisfied that I am doing the right thing.' Craig, Paisley, and Desmond Boal, MP for Shankill, were not sure. Indeed the acceptance by West of a seat in Faulkner's cabinet enraged and disappointed them. The government's potential opponents were well and truly split now. With West in the Cabinet there was also Captain John Brooke, Mr John Taylor and in government, a new position of Parliamentary Secretary to the Ministry of Health and Social Service was given to Mr Joe Burns, a right-wing hardliner from North Derry whose opposition to every reform in the past had been tempered because of his inability to express himself in any other than gut phrases on the Twelfth of July. But the important thing for Faulkner was that all these men represented rural constituencies. The government now had roots in nearly every rural area where opposition was expected. As a balance to West the post of Minister of Community Relations went outside parliament to Mr David Bleakley, a former Labour MP for Victoria. This was represented in the lobbies to unsuspecting British journalists as a major move of reforming significance.

Whatever about Bleakley's personal qualities and appeal – and throughout his term of office which could only last six months under provision of the Government of Ireland Act 1920 – many would testify to his hard work and almost untiring efforts to do his best – the office of Minister of Community Relations was a gimmick and no personality under the sun would have made it less so. It was an office which did little except by way of social welfare, said much but was more often than not unlistened to, and generally it summed up the central dilemma facing any government in a divided society like Northern Ireland: it is one thing to legislate for community peace, it is another thing to get that peace or to make people work towards it.

21

If the office of Minister of Community Relations had a value it was that it showed up the inherent problem of trying to improve community relations in Northern Ireland. Bleakley's appointment gave Faulkner a sort of coalition government and was represented as the taste of things to come. The new Minister immediately set off on a personal campaign of hard work and there is no evidence to suggest that he was ever under the Orange–Unionist influence while in office. But it would be difficult now to point to any single thing the office achieved in Bleakley's six months and there seems more sense in the suggestion that appointing him was an effort by Faulkner to demonstrate that Stormont and its government could work if it gave a little here and there. Already in the appointment of the Labour man Faulkner was launched on the save-Stormont policy.

Faulkner's style was evident too in the missing names: Phelim O'Neill and Dr Robert Simpson had both gone, two supporters of reform biting the political dust. True, neither man had particularly wanted to serve Faulkner but there was no pressure put on them to stay and help or to stay and give a liberal flavour to the new Cabinet. And from the 'liberal' wing of Unionism, now that it had lost Mr Robin Bailie who went into the new government as Minister of Commerce, there was only one small gesture : Mrs Anne Dickson, MP for Carrick and a supporter, though not a very vocal one, of O'Neill and Chichester-Clark, resigned the Parliamentary Whip because of West's inclusion in the new team. She wasn't joined in her stance or encouraged in it by anyone else. It was a measure of Faulkner's qualities as a manager that in his first few moves he had convinced a wide cross-section of people that what he was doing was not only fair, right and reasonable but that it was hopeful too for the future. He was, by any stretch of the imagination, off to a very good start. Whenever commentators at the time pointed to the anomalies and contradictions in his government appointments he just waited the few days necessary for this to blow over and carried on regardless. And in particular what he had done in those first days was a great boost for Unionist party unity. What it would mean for the rest of Northern Ireland would only be seen gradually.

A few days after his announcement of the cabinet Faulkner got a three to one majority in a vote of confidence at the Unionist Party Standing Committee meeting in Belfast.

Against all this Paisley asked whether there was any honesty left in Northern politics; John McQuade, MP for Woodvale, attacked West for joining the cabinet; and even Bill Craig who had given Faulkner a chance was saying after the meeting that the Government would 'probably not have support in the constituencies'. But whether he heard them or not Faulkner showed not the slightest sign of paying any attention to his critics on either side of the fence. He was pressing ahead with the job on hand and the work was being done crisply, evenly and with remarkably little fuss. By the end of the month he had declared an amnesty for privately-held guns and had emphasised that even legally-held guns should, where they weren't needed, be handed in to police stations or military posts. The amnesty would last until 8 April, he said. In the Commons at Stormont he followed up his success with the Standing Committee by getting a vote of confidence for his new administration. He was even more firmly on the road now.

He definitely got a breather too from the streets. Looked at in relation to what had happened in the first three months and in March particularly, April and May were quiet. The Republican Easter parades passed off peacefully with only minor rioting in the Protestant Newtownards Road after a local Orange parade. In May the big Ulster '71' Exhibition which had been planned for years opened in Belfast quietly and crowds, while not as big as had been hoped, began to stream to Botanic Gardens to see it. Admittedly the atmosphere in Belfast, and Derry especially, was still tense. But there had been no dramatically visible signs of a harder line from the Prime Minister and the only ominous signs were bomb attacks on the homes of some RUC special branch men in the Belfast area and a daylight bomb on the Protestant Shankill Road which only just missed killing or causing at least serious injuries to early customers. A few people were hurt but only slightly. But May was to have a very nasty sting in its tail which was to rock Faulkner very hard and leave him shaken for the first time in his two months of office. It happened almost casually.

After the Newtownards Road riots Faulkner himself had visited Mount Pottinger RUC station to speak to troops and police on the ground. Another minor riot had developed around his presence and as his car was leaving stones and bottles were thrown at it but the Prime Minister wasn't hurt. There was some gunfire in the area too and a police sergeant was hit in the leg. At first the shooting was, naturally enough in some quarters, put down to the IRA but when a day later the Army officially apologised saying it had been one of their men who fired and whose bullet had ricocheted, the small incident began to assume larger importance. The question was arising bluntly for the first time under Faulkner: when and in what circumstances will the soldiers open fire? Troops in the North are equipped with a Ministry of Defence yellow card with firing instructions but, apart from the first few weeks in August 1969, that document is not worth the reinforced paper it is typed on.

What was being built up to towards the end of May had other roots too: notably the killing of an IRA man William Reid by troops, rioting at Gallaher's Factory in North Queen Street and attacks on police stations, police landrovers and other expressions of violence in the community. Reid had been stopped by soldiers when they recognised the car he was in with two other men had been stolen. The car occupants and the military exchanged fire, Reid was killed, his two companions injured and two soldiers also hit by gunfire. At Gallaher's young Catholic girls were abused and intimidated by the mainly Protestant work force because they had, it was claimed, attended Reid's IRA style funeral through the streets of Belfast. As a result of incidents of this type military patrols in Belfast for the first time began to be strengthened: landrovers roamed in twos, the single soldier who had kept lookout at the back now became two, one man facing forward, one keeping check at the rear. There were machine-gun attacks along the M1 motorway at army vehicles and there was a general quickening in the tempo of activity. But worse was to come. Just before the House of Commons rose on Tuesday night, 25 May, Faulkner, replying to an adjournment debate, issued a strong warning to the 'whole community' that the security forces would be tough and clamp down on those responsible for such activities as had been seen in the previous days. Then he added: 'Any soldier seeing any person with a weapon or acting suspiciously may, depending on the circumstances, fire to warn or with effect without waiting for orders.'

The statement quite literally brought gasps from the Opposition benches. And Faulkner followed up by saying that on the Monday night previously the policy had been put into action when troops opened fire on a car, which they had recognised as stolen, when it failed to stop at a roadblock. Outside in the corridors of Stormont Mr Paddy Devlin, MP for Falls and Mr Austin Currie, MP for East Tyrone, the two remaining SDLP MPs in the House at the time, made their position absolutely clear: 'If authority is now being put into the hands of soldiers, who for example consider Catholics responsible for murdering three Scottish soldiers, to shoot to kill at anything that moves, then we will withdraw from Parliament. We could not stay in a Parliament which would put that authority into the hands of soldiers. In the absence of a satisfactory explanation we will withdraw from Stormont.' Mr Currie however added that he would not be surprised if the Prime Minister was 'word-spinning'. He added: 'We will get a watered-down version in a day or two.' A matter of an hour after Faulkner spoke a member of the Provisional IRA walked across the lower Springfield Road in Belfast, lobbed a suitcase at the front door of the RUC station and ran away. The suitcase contained fifty pounds of gelignite. An extremely brave soldier, Sergeant Michael Willets of the Parachute Regiment, ushered some women and children who were near the door to safety. Then the bomb went off and he was blown to pieces. The front of the station was wrecked. Politics and the security scene went to bed that night with ominous sleeping tablets. The next day the trouble really began.

By Wednesday afternoon it was clear that whatever breathing space Faulkner had been given by either side his position as Premier was under serious question for the first time. In the Commons he was closely questioned following a private notice question from Mr Paddy Kennedy, Republican Labour MP for Central, in whose constituency the Gallaher rioting and the death of Reid had taken place. The exchanges were bitter and in many respects the worst in the House for some years. The Prime Minister said that when he had used the words 'acting suspiciously' he had quite obviously meant circumstances in which firearms or explosives were being or might be used. Then he added: 'The situation where the man who carried death and destruction to Springfield Road RUC station last night is the type of situation I and the Army had in mind when I spoke on Tuesday.' The Opposition were further infuriated by this, since Faulkner's original statement had been made before that explosion. And particularly since the Army had denied that there was any change in their tactics or their orders.

Faulkner was in fact acting completely in accord with military advice and on their intelligence when he spoke on Tuesday in the Commons. Some of his security advisers had had a routine meeting with Major General Tony Farrar-Hockley the Commander of Land Forces for a discussion of the serious situation which was escalating even before the previous weekend. Based on that meeting one of Faulkner's aides had written out the lines about firing on suspicion and had made doubly sure with Farrar-Hockley that this was correct. He had been assured it was and even when the row broke over the Faulkner statement another check had been made.

Again the aide was assured that what the Prime Minister had said was accurate and reflected army policy. Soldiers could fire at their own discretion if they thought the circumstances warranted it. At the time the Army's version of events was accepted as accurate because its press office was considered slightly more reliable than Faulkner himself. In fact Faulkner was saying what they had advised him to say and the Army was trying to wriggle out of a tricky political situation. The impact this had on Faulkner was important. He was personally upset by it, showed his upset by downright nastiness in the Commons when answering questions and generally the atmosphere was soured by the incident. The bitterness and tension between Faulkner and the Opposition which were there beneath the surface had become obvious. And Faulkner was just two months in office. In the corridors at Stormont even supporters of the Premier were unsettled by the incident. Now, after the weeks of support from Unionist constituencies, the apparent easing in the security situation, the votes of confidence and the closing of party ranks, the first flaws in his rule were emerging. If he had had the type of personality that could admit when he was wrong or – as in this case – when he had been misled, he could have got over the crisis. But the trouble was, as it had been and would continue to be to the end, that distrust of Faulkner was growing right across the board in the Northern community.

This gap was now seen to the full. Basically Faulkner was never trusted by the Catholic people in Northern Ireland. Nor, indeed, after his full identification with the Hunt Report disbanding the B Specials and disarming the police, did his opinion count for much among Protestant grass-root and working-class opinion either. Austin Currie once summed up the reactions of Catholics: 'The trouble with Brian Faulkner is that if the Catholics asked him to stand on his head for them and he agreed they would still say "rat"'. That was the way it was from his first entry into politics. But there was also an effort on his part, from 1969 onwards, to identify with reform. He had assured the 'loyalist' people that the Specials would not be disbanded but had had their demise voted through the House of Commons having agreed to it at the Downing Street meeting in August. He had stood by the former premier Chichester-Clark until the very last moment and no-one in the community had really pondered the question : why? As most supporters of Chichester-Clark said, it didn't seem to matter why Faulkner was supporting reform; what mattered was that he was doing it and he seemed pretty good at it. As Minister of Development he cut an impressive figure and drew grudging laughs one day, even from the Opposition, when, after praise had been heaped on him for some performance or other he said : 'In my Ministry the difficult we do at once, the impossible takes a little longer'. But from those near-heady days when the world had seemed to revolve around his capabilities, things had begun to fall away a few months after he first took office as Premier.

As the days passed he became more and more of a loner, with fewer friends even inside his cabinet. It is true that in the end it was events which were to be the ruin of Stormont, events like internment, the withdrawal of the Opposition, the 'Bloody Sunday' killings in Derry and many others besides. But the downfall of the parliament and government of Northern Ireland is inextricably bound up in the style, the personality and the political career and beliefs of Brian Faulkner. It is as if at least most of the roads to downfall lead from him. He has speed, flexibility to a point of being a chameleon and a positive relish for politics. When Chichester-Clark was under severe pressure Faulkner would take on the job of government 'talker' appearing on television, talking on radio programmes and giving interviews and off-the-record chats to reporters from home and abroad. At such things he was superb : he could talk his own way and the way of the Northern Ireland government out of any situation no matter what the facts said. Inside the Unionist party he

28

had shown some remarkable courage. He attacked dissidents bitterly, stood up to the attacks on government policies which he supported and lambasted critics of the Chichester-Clark administration. And at his ministry, as Phelim O'Neill once said in the Commons: 'Legislation flies in and out of it at a speed that leaves one standing.' But there were too many skeletons in his cupboard for the Catholics to give him anything but grudging, temporary support. And the Protestants had cause for hating him too. Even if they didn't go quite as far as Paisley in dubbing him the 'little shirtmaker', many of them did not trust him very far.

The skeletons were there to be dragged from Twelfth of July platforms when the Prime Minister in various roles had made blatantly anti-Catholic speeches, even to the extent of suggesting that the film the *Song of Bernadette* should not be circulated in Northern Ireland because it showed the Catholic clergy in a favourable light. One didn't have to go quite that far to find cause for suspicion. He had the misfortune to look shifty and nothing he did belied that appearance. His political contortions too were legendary. He had resigned from O'Neill's government allegedly because he thought the Captain was slow on reform and if that hadn't been so dishonest it might have been funny. A week or two later he was challenging James Chichester-Clark for the premiership and openly canvassing support for a return to pre-1968 days. His political friends had once been on the Right, then he courted the Left and finally he tried the centre. He is a man whose only concern is the maintenance of Unionist power in Northern Ireland at any cost. Every move he made while Prime Minister was aimed precisely at that and not a single thing he did would in any way have altered the power block of his party and his government, so long as the system lasted. In other words, as he had demonstrated in his first words on taking up the leadership of the Parliamentary party. Faulkner was ultimately a *status quo* man. If he had a political dictum it was: you give a little, you stay in power. He ended giving hardly anything and losing all power. He was a man who could create the appearance of change when in fact there was no change at all. He had a way with words. In Britain there is every evidence to suggest that he went down well. Some commentators seemed to think that he was sufficiently good to be exported for high office in Westminster, and even reliable papers such as the *Guardian* and the *Economist* could at times go quite overboard about his ability. At home he was supported by the Unionist *Newsletter*, attacked repeatedly by the Catholic *Irish News* and though occasionally given the benefit of the doubt by the *Belfast Telegraph* he was condemned there too. It strongly attacked, for example, the crude politicking in the formation of his cabinet.

As a Stormont Prime Minister therefore Faulkner had some things going for him and some positive and massive disadvantages. To begin with, the resignation of Chichester-Clark had wakened Westminster out of its lethargy momentarily and although Faulkner didn't get very visible new support he was a more persuasive arguer and a more determined fighter than his predecessor. There were constant reminders from his aides during his term of office that there was a 'special relationship' between himself and Edward Heath. As well, in his first few days and even weeks, things had been fairly quiet. Everybody, it seemed, was giving him a chance. But as the situation changed and the emerging Provisional IRA began to intensify operations his nerves, of all things, began to fray. The 'shoot to kill on suspicion' order – not so much because Faulkner gave it, but because he refused to clear up the misunderstanding it created – was a classic case in point. He often lost his temper in the House. One of Faulkner's main disadvantages was his background. If he had really wanted to offer the hand of reconciliation then a dramatic gesture like resigning from the Orange Order of which he remained a member during his full term of office would have been not merely a help, but a massive indication of how he felt things should have been moving. Rightly or wrongly the Orange set-up is far more ugly to the Catholic population than it is attractive to the mass of Protestants. That is to say that the support Faulkner would have gained among the Catholics by resigning would have far outweighed any 'Protestant backlash' against him for doing so. He stayed put. He had once told a planning conference in Newcastle in the late sixties when he was Minister of Commerce that it was a 'crying shame that religion and politics should be intertwined'. He never showed in his premiership that he thought continued membership of the Orange Order was not just a crying shame but a positive and genuine block to progress. For a man of supposedly high capabilities he seldom matched his promises with action.

Among the Protestant community as has been noted his identification with the 'reform' programme had cost him dear. It must have seemed to him unfair that he took the odium for being so identified and never got any corresponding confidence from the Catholics as he might have had a right to expect. But that was the gap, the credibility gap, the gap of trust. One comes back time and time again in Northern Ireland to the dictum that appearances are more important than reality.

Faulkner seemed shifty, untrustworthy and a chameleon. He had the opportunities to show that he wasn't these things but refused to take them. He conducted much of his time as Prime Minister as if he were managing a high-powered company rather than trying to govern a very sensitive community with massive problems. He behaved as if Northern Ireland needed no help from anywhere and as if it, under his leadership, could solve its own problems. He made a personal crusade of trying to win every battle, the security one being at the forefront of his mind. And as time went on he took on more and more and every move was characterised by his own personal style. Thus the appointment of a Catholic to the cabinet would, when it was announced, be presented by him as a major and significant move rather than as a slight, hopeful sign backed up with precious little else. Thus, his government's Green Paper with the most ludicrous ideas for expanding the House of Commons at a time when most sides in Northern Ireland were agreed that it was less politics, not more, that people wanted, would be presented as another major step in the move forward. All these things were to come and more besides.

But as Sergeant Willet's funeral moved past Springfield Road RUC station on Friday 28 May a new and vital turn had been taken in the political life of the Stormont parliament. Its foundations had become even more unsteady in the space of a few days.

3 FAULKNER OFFERS: OPPOSITION REJECTS

On Tuesday, 1 June, Irish newspapers carried a long report of a speech by Mr John Hume, SDLP MP for Foyle, in which he called for an end to the Government of Ireland Act 1920 and the system of government which it created and a willingness from the British government to create a new system in which sectarianism would be neutralised and in which all sections of the Northern Ireland community could participate at every level. Hume, speaking at a meeting of his local SDLP executive, said that he would like to see the British government declare the new system as a principle and invite all interested groups to submit proposals. 'Only then can we begin to create a united and prosperous community,' he said. Hume went on to say that he believed the logic of the British intervention in 1969 had never been faced, particularly by Britain herself. He went on: 'The arrival of British troops to maintain law and order, the forcing by the Westminster government of a reform programme on Stormont and the continuing presence of British watchdogs is the clearest possible public admission that the Unionist government are and were incapable of governing Northern Ireland in peace, justice and stability. Their intervention when allied to the continuing presence of a Unionist government has created a situation of permanent instability in Northern Ireland and we have no less than three Prime Ministers in two years to prove it.' He summed up by warning his audience that 'no-one can underestimate the serious dangers inherent in the present situation in Northern Ireland'. And it was clear in this and other speeches by Hume and his colleagues that these dangers were not just in the security field.

For the next few days politicians in the North and in Britain had something new to argue about: it was mooted

33

that there was a proposal for a full-time battalion of the unfortunately named Ulster Defence Regiment. The regiment had been the recommendation of the Hunt Report and had come into force on 1 April. Its purpose was not so much to replace the B men as to become a unit within the British Army and, unlike the Specials, it would therefore be under army control; its prime aim, however, would be to guard key installations and patrol the border. It had been made clear by the British government that 'it was not the intention to use the UDR in street rioting' and news that there might now be a full-time squad raised grave suspicions in Opposition minds. It seemed at the time possible that a full-time unit would be formed. The arguments were strong against the idea : in the Commons at Stormont a bitter question time was spent arguing the toss. Opposition MPs said the idea was to placate the Unionist right-wing and whether or not this was so, that side of the Unionist party certainly gave tentative backing to the idea. Mr Faulkner, replying in the House, said that the two governments were determined to take any initiative necessary to end the campaign of violence by the IRA and every avenue would be explored. The issue and the debate ended there for the time being. But the effect had been to intensify the sharpness of the exchanges between the government and the Opposition and to give further cause for concern among non-parliamentary anti-Unionist groups. Within days the idea of the full-time battalion had been accepted and the argument was one of when rather than whether.

There was a second distraction, for it was no more, in that second week in June. Orangemen who had planned a march in the 90 per cent Catholic town of Dungiven had been told by the authorities to cancel their procession. They decided to go ahead in defiance. On the Sunday at the bridge outside the town over the river Roe hundreds of Orangemen clashed with British troops and CS gas and rubber bullets were fired to disperse them. Several arrests were made and the incident, while it embarrassed Faulkner in Unionist and Orange circles, marginally caught the anti-Unionist forces on the wrong foot: the authorities had an anti-Protestant action to use if they were ever to be accused of partiality in the exercise of their powers. The Dungiven incident was petty and despite contemporary mutterings from Orange hardliners it blew over almost as quickly as the CS gas used against the brethren. If Dungiven did mean anything it was that further marches by the Orangemen were put in doubt for the first time. On an RTE interview Faulkner said that he 'hoped the major traditional parades' could go ahead as planned but it was by no means certain. Still, when a week later the first of the big urban processions was planned it was allowed to take place with only minor rerouting. This was the Orange march from the Shankill Road to Whiterock Orange Hall. It had been described as traditional by Orangemen. It was in fact just ten years old, a mere newcomer by Orange standards; the previous year, after it had passed dangerously close to the Catholic-Protestant peace line along Cupar Street, major rioting followed and rapidly spread all over the city, and six people were killed. This time however, despite some grim forecasts, the march passed off peacefully. The security forces were out in strength and there were only minor incidents. But attacks on police stations continued, several people were shot in Belfast, and there were other minor incidents throughout the North. Nevertheless, the three weeks of June that had passed were by any standards peaceful and apart from political rows of not very major importance the atmosphere seemed tranquil once more. It was precisely at this point that Brian Faulkner tried his first major move since becoming Prime Minister. In his statement on taking office he had promised to hold early talks with all shades of opinion – and he emphasised all – and promised equally to listen to what such opinion would have to say. 'Indeed,' he had said, 'I shall place great emphasis on keeping the community in the picture. I aim to have a government that is frank with the people, with no punches pulled and no glossing over of difficulties.' He was now about to try and put some of this into action. Or rather into some more

35

words, for what he was thinking of amounted not so much to new departures as to the promise of new departures. The occasion he chose was during his reply to the debate on the Queen's speech. On Tuesday 22 June he told the Stormont Commons that he had decided to set up three new functional committees of the Commons covering the fields of social, environmental and industrial services. They would be set up if the House agreed before the end of the year and he added that at least two of the new committees would have Opposition MPs as chairmen. These chairmen would be paid. They would have nine members each, based on representation in the Commons at the time, and their principal function would be the consideration of major proposals of policy, the review of performance and the consideration of legislation. It was, said Faulkner, an indication of his government's intention to involve all the people of Northern Ireland, politicians included, in participation in the running of their own affairs. He added an appeal to all political interests to meet him for 'frank and wideranging discussions broadly-based, representative of the full spectrum of views in both houses of parliament, aimed at seeking some measure of common ground in restoring peace and stability and resuming social and economic advance'. Conscious of a decline in confidence in the community Mr Faulkner told a press briefing that he was anxious for a good unanimous response to his ideas because his government was anxious that people in Northern Ireland should 'come again to look to parliament for confidence and leadership'. 'Short of asking the Opposition to run the country this is the best means of participation for them,' he said. The proposals were given a welcome in the Commons by Gerry Fitt and were attacked in strong terms by Ian Paisley. There was full and thoughtful coverage in most of the local media and something akin to hysteria in the British press. But looked at soberly the plans were nothing like what they had been made out to be by Faulkner.

The proposals were in fact merely an effort by Faulkner to get Opposition assistance in his bid to keep Stormont alive and operational. There was a feeling in the air that the parliament was on increasingly shaky ground and this, together with the nagging memory that the British intervention of 1969 had been dramatic and potentially of vital significance for Stormont's life-span, provided a strong sense of urgency about the rescue operation. Faulkner was shrewd enough to realise that this could never be effected without Opposition assistance. Their support was absolutely and clearly essential to the continuance of Stormont. But the committee idea was a gimmick. It proposed nothing at all that would in any way interfere with Unionist hegemony. There would be committees but their membership would be in proportion to the make-up of the present legislature, in other words Unionist-dominated. They would have no legislative or executive powers, but would exist solely as advisory bodies. They would have Opposition chairmen but that made no difference either except that while Unionists were agreeing how to vote the Opposition representatives would be trying to arrange the meetings and do the work. And, most pointless of all, they would consider 'major proposals of policy, the review of performance and the consideration of legislation'. In a parliament of fifty-two members, not all of them regular attenders, the idea of paring down that number to consider anything is in itself almost a joke. But in a devolved, regional parliament with no control over these very aspects of government the thought was either pure Alice-In-Wonderland or a political trick.

It was of course the latter. The Prime Minister knew that on examination, which he hoped would not be too thorough, the ideas would not stand up. There was little enough at Stormont to keep the House of Commons going never mind three new committees. But he hoped that by attracting the Opposition and giving them the appearance of involvement he could place them in a position where the maintenance of the system would be as much in their interest as it was in his. That, nothing more nor less, was what was behind the committee offer. It was dressed up of course in fine words, some of the finest used for a long

37

time, and it took the Opposition by surprise. The Prime Minister delivered it superbly at the Dispatch Box, giving every impressive word full emphasis and attracting the suitable quota of 'hear, hears' from cabinet and back benches. Gerry Fitt was quickly on his feet to say he gave a guarded welcome to the proposals; he hadn't seen them fully of course and he couldn't commit his party, but they sounded at first hearing worth a second look and he hoped his party would be at least able to co-operate. Fitt went on: 'We are not at this point in time going to give our allegiance completely to the Prime Minister unless we can see that he really intends to put his words into action.' And as he ended his speech, not having referred in any part of it to the recurrence of violence, allegations of Army misbehaviour and especially to the recent 'shoot on suspicion' statement by Faulkner, the SDLP leader said: 'As I said earlier we have had two Queen's speeches this afternoon. By far the more important was the speech made at the Dispatch Box by the Prime Minister, in which he indicated to the House that he is prepared to engage in new activities. He mentioned participation and asked for the support of all responsible people in the community and for the support of the Opposition here. He said that his door will be open if we feel there is anything constructive we can put to him. We will go into his words very carefully this evening and we certainly hope to take him up on the challenge he has thrown out to the whole community.' Fitt sat down and there was no indication whatever that he had anything in mind other than what he had said: the SDLP would look at the proposals and they hoped to be able to co-operate.

Paisley followed Fitt and immediately attacked the Prime Minister and the proposals. He demanded, not for the first time, a general election, pointing out to the House that the country had now got to its second Prime Minister without an election and saying that the policies proposed had no support from the people and the government no mandate. He was very telling too on one point – the committees themselves: 'This is a small parliament and there is plenty of time to debate in committee. In view of the sparseness of attendance at committee stages I wonder how many would be present at a committee of nine if, with the membership of the House, we can sometimes hardly have a quorum at certain committees.'

The debate adjourned for the day after Paisley had finished. Hume did not speak until well into the second day. He had had ample time to study Faulkner's speech and, as he was considered to have one of the best brains in the party, it was expected that none of the implications in the proposals would escape his notice. He was sceptical in places, in other points in his speech he was offering some co-operation. He said: 'What about the proposals in the speech itself? Some of these proposals were pitched as major concessions to the Opposition, and indeed to the minority as a whole. Let me say at once that the proposals dealing with the formation of committees of this House are not new. Let me put it on the record and make it clear that from this side of the House there went to the Macrory committee, which was investigating the re-organisation of local government, a set of proposals on the re-organisation of local government which included the setting up of such committees.' He went on to say that the idea of the committees was 'essential if centralisation is to work'. At the time local government power was being centralised and agencies like the Central Housing Executive were coming into being. Hume pointed out too that there would still be a majority of Unionists on the committees and warned that they could negative any work done. He asked for further details about the nature, scope and powers of Faulkner's proposals. At another part of his speech Hume said of Faulkner's speech: '. . . they are fine words and we will match them with equally fine words. But we would want to see fine actions following those words and then we will equally match the actions of the Prime Minister and his government with our actions.'

At one point in his speech Hume attacked the Orange Order link with the Unionist party and particularly pointed out that the party which supported the government of the day had just previously found itself unable to break the links with the Orangemen. This was a reference to the committee within the Unionist party which, under the Attorney-General Mr Basil Kelly, had been set up a year previously by Chichester-Clark to 'study party organisation'. Although it suggested some minor changes in the representation of groups in the party structure, the report of this committee did not make any suggestion that the Orange representation should be altered. The block delegate-representation of the Order within the party would be maintained. 'There exists', he said, 'this essential contradiction in the connection between the Orange Order and the Unionist party which must make us on this side of the House cautious about any promises that come from the government.' But perhaps there are two quotes from Hume's speech which indicate more clearly that, despite his guarded reception for the precise proposals, he was by no means reluctant to assist in the betterment of the Stormont system. 'It should be made clear to all people today who say that no change has taken place that this is simply not true. There have been changes in this community and there must be more changes, but it takes time before legislative change becomes reality in the lives of the people and if people interfere with the progress of that change by violence, they only increase the frustration.'

And a few paragraphs further on he had this to say: 'What has failed in Northern Ireland other than the system no-one wanted? Surely that is the lesson that is staring us in the face, and are the confines of our discussion on the problems of Northern Ireland not too narrow? Should we not be discussing the system itself rather than tinkering with it any further?' He went on to talk about ultimate Irish unity but it is clear from the lack of emphasis he placed on this part of his speech that nothing was further from his mind at the time than putting forward anything concrete to follow up his speech earlier in the month in which he had called for an end to the Government of Ireland Act 1920 and the system it had created. If Hume, the most articulate and in many ways the shrewdest SDLP spokesman around, was willing to give the Faulkner proposals a try then it was clear that the party was committed to working within the contemporary system. Faulkner must have been happy with the first signs from the Opposition : outright rejection of his proposals would have been disastrous, anything short of rejection would have been hopeful, but the attitude of the SDLP was such that he must have had reasonable grounds for believing that his plans would work. And if that was to happen then another helping hand would be given to his government in its efforts to maintain itself and the institution of Stormont. There was a faint possibility that the unsteady foundations of a few weeks earlier would be restored – with a bonus.

When Austin Currie spoke it was to move an amendment to the main resolution. It called the government's ideas only 'a tinkering with the system which is not relevant to the exceptional conditions of political life in Northern Ireland', and called for the 'setting up of a select committee for the purposes of recommending the necessary institutional and procedural changes'. In other words, the party had looked at Faulkner's ideas and even in the light of Hume's speech in Derry, of his use of the word 'tinkering' (and it turned up in the amendment proposed by Currie) and of the party's own guarded welcome to the ideas, there was no indication whatever that its thinking was directed along lines which would lead to a demand for the end of the system. By the time Paddy Devlin spoke near-hysteria had set into the SDLP. He called Faulkner's speech 'his best hour since he became Prime Minister', and this wasn't intended as a smart remark to the two-month reign of the Premier. It was serious. And Devlin also said : 'I feel the Prime Minister is right in his approach. He realises the nonsense of trying to attract that lot on his back benches. He is not going to the right-wing any more. He is going to the middle ground to attract and make friends with the people in the middle ground, knowing that at the next election it is very likely he will get the Alliance vote, the NICRA vote (Northern

Ireland Civil Rights Association), the vote of all the decent people in the community.'

When Fitt got his chance to speak a second time he summed up his party's attitude : 'At this stage in the development of the state we are prepared to say that we will accept the promises of the Prime Minister, that we are prepared to co-operate with the government to prevent a further tragic loss of life and that we are prepared to take any steps we can in conformity with the government to prevent hundreds of innocent men, women and children, Protestants and Catholics, being maimed as they have been over the past two or three years.' Faulkner was delighted with the debate. He called it 'the best and most responsible debate we have had in this House for a great many years' and he complimented without exception every Opposition spokesman who had contributed. He suggested this reflected opinion in the country as a whole. He was interrupted once by Currie who asked: 'Are you going to accept the amendment?' but in the main his speech went smoothly until at the end he was able to ask the SDLP not to press their amendment to a vote. 'In view of all that I have said I would ask the movers of the amendment not to press it to a division. I would ask honourable members on all benches to give earnest thought to these matters during the recess and to be ready to make a contribution to the wide-ranging debate which I have proposed when we resume after the recess. If the debate over the last three days is any indication then I would be very optimistic indeed about the outcome of our deliberation in the autumn' (Hon. Members : Hear, hear).

And Faulkner got his wish : nodding heads from Gerry Fitt and other SDLP members indicated their willingness to call off putting their amendment to a vote and the official report records that this debate ended with the pro-government motion being 'put and agreed to . . . Resolved : nemine contradicente'. Faulkner now had the stated willingness of the entire Opposition to give him a chance to make a departure within the Stormont system work. Everyone went home that Thursday night, after three days of debate, feeling that even if the old political acrimony would be resumed next week at least there seemed the basis for government/opposition co-operation. It was, if not the Prime Minister's finest hour, certainly his best success since taking office. He had won the Opposition with words and they in their turn had every reason to think that the government was not far from agreeing to repeated Opposition demands for proportional representation for any future general elections. Yet he was the man who had resigned from O'Neill's government because of the setting-up of the Cameron Commission; he had not enthused over the setting-up of the Hunt Report and Scarman was not his idea either. Even in his speech he had mentioned that he thought one of the failures of the government in recent years had been their desire to bring in outside experts 'to the devaluation of this parliament'. Most people would agree that if the three above-mentioned 'outside experts' had not been called in the Brian Faulkners of Northern Ireland would have been a long time getting ahead with any reform whatever.

It was accepted then that, whatever about the precise details of his plans, at least Faulkner's speech in the Commons had a tone of reconciliation about it. The words used were hopeful, according to the best Opposition judgement of them, and if the future still held chaos those few days after the debate on the Queen's speech were full of speculation about how the committee would work, whether the Opposition would take a salary for chairmanship, what fields they would cover, how they could be extended and so on. So June ended on a note of hope.

On Monday 28 June, those hopes were seriously threatened. After an Orange parade in Lurgan, Co. Armagh, local leaders of the Order adjourned to nearby headquarters at Brownlow House where some of them were surprised to find the most senior officers of the Orange and Black and Apprentice Boy organisations waiting for a meeting. Soon afterwards the Stormont Prime Minister Mr Faulkner and several senior cabinet colleagues arrived.

They met the Orange leaders and their colleagues and the meeting lasted several hours. It was stated afterwards that neither the Premier nor his cabinet had in any way given in to or made a deal with the Orangemen about any aspect of government. This appears to be true: there was little to make a deal about at the time since Faulkner was riding pretty high, the security forces were apparently tougher than they had been, and the Opposition seemed at least acquiescent and at best positively co-operative. Faulkner held the whip hand at the meeting, was severely critical of the Dungiven affair and while he gave almost an assurance that the big July Twelfth demonstrations would go ahead he warned too about misbehaviour.

After the 'Lurgan Parliament' as Austin Currie quickly dubbed the meeting the Opposition attacked Faulkner in the Commons. John Hume asked: 'How does the Prime Minister expect any of us to have any confidence in the impartiality of either himself or his government in dealing with Orange marches when we had the pathetic sight of half a cabinet being summoned to a secret society last night to be told what to do?' But Hume and the SDLP only complained about the meeting in the context of Orange marches. There was, surprisingly, little debate as to whether or not the meeting had undermined Faulkner's credibility on other matters as well. Faulkner parried the attack in great style: 'Far from it being a shame that I and some of my colleagues should go to that meeting we did the responsible thing in making it clear to people who were organising parades this year what precisely is the government's policy towards parades.' It was certainly a misfortune that this hadn't been done either publicly or at Stormont Castle. It left in many minds, though apparently not in the mind of the SDLP, the awkward feeling that even if Faulkner had spoken some hard words to the Orangemen something else might have been agreed too. It was an unfortunate, and ill-timed meeting. Brian Faulkner should have known better and when he looked back on it he must have been relieved and surprised that he got off so lightly.

On Wednesday 7 July, Faulkner held a meeting with MPs from all parties at Stormont. When they entered – a most comical array, incidentally, with Paddy Devlin cheek by jowl with Bill Craig – Faulkner asked them to agree that nothing should be leaked to the press, and that they would decide on a statement which would be issued after the meeting. They muttered consent and then, in the course of the meeting, he offered for common signature a piece of paper on which was written an agreement that all discussions of a political nature between the government and Opposition would take place only if Northern Ireland's position within the United Kingdom was accepted by all parties. Only Craig agreed to sign. There was no mention from the Opposition of the Brownlow House meeting and indeed the only person to bring it up was Phelim O'Neill, former Minister and by now a thorn in the government's side from the backbenches. He criticised it on sectarian grounds. Austin Currie agreed. The matter was glossed over by Faulkner and left at that. Afterwards a statement agreed by all participants said: 'We have had today the first meeting of representatives of various parties and interests in the House of Commons. Nothing of this sort – involving private and completely frank exchanges – has been attempted before. It is not to be expected that anything in the nature of concrete decisions or proposals could emerge from the first such meeting. What is important is that the meeting has been approached by everyone in a helpful and constructive spirit and as a result the position taken on a number of issues has been clarified. We all think it worthwhile to continue with this experiment in patient discussion and intend to meet again for further talks.' The SDLP agreed to this statement.

It was becoming increasingly clear at this stage that the party was still committed to working within the system. Co-operation was building up between Faulkner and his old friend Gerry Fitt. Fitt and his party were happy. Things were looking up. But the day after that meeting the situation on the ground deteriorated drastically. Derry, where there had been rioting and violence

45

of one kind or another for most of the week, had come to the boil. Since the Monday there had been persistent gun and nail-bomb attacks on troops and running riots between soldiers and Bogsiders. In the afternoon of Thursday 8th, and the early hours of the Friday morning, two young Derry men, Desmond Beattie and Seamus Cusack were shot dead by soldiers. Cusack in fact was shot in the leg and died in a Donegal hospital from loss of blood; he had been taken there rather than to a local hospital because his friends were anxious to avoid military road-blocks. On Thursday afternoon the Commons rose for the summer recess and Faulkner ended the session with a prayer that out of the 'evil of Derry there may come some good for the whole community'. What he meant was anybody's guess, but it was a pretty meaningless phrase. The near-euphoria that had been in the house a few weeks and even a few days earlier was rapidly evaporated. Soon it would be gone altogether when John Hume, having made exhaustive inquiries in Derry, announced himself dissatisfied with the Army version of how the two men died.

On Friday 9 July Hume said : 'I personally publicly challenge the British Army to face an inquiry which will prove that they are telling lies about these deaths.' What the Army said was expected, and was to become more expected as the year went on : the two men were armed and that was why they were shot. There was no further explanation or clarification given. At a hastily summoned press conference the C.O. of the troops involved, Lieutenant Colonel Roy Jackson, said : 'Both men were armed. There is no possibility whatsoever that my soldiers could have made a mistake. I would point out that since Sunday last my men have been fired on every night, attacked with nail bombs and other missiles and that only on Wednesday did we fire back. One of these men had a nail bomb, the other man was levelling a rifle to fire at soldiers. That is why they were shot.' By now Ivan Cooper had called the situation in Derry the 'most serious for years' and Eddie McAteer, who has one of the best tongues in Northern Ireland for expressing himself in short, pithy and often sardonic phrases, said bluntly what many in the Bogside were thinking : 'Protocol be damned. Directly or indirectly Dublin must take effective action in the protection of their Northern people.'

Meanwhile the SDLP were spread around the country. Devlin had taken off for Dublin to attend the Truce celebrations in the city, Hume and Cooper were in the Bogside, Currie was at home in Coalisland, O'Hanlon in Armagh, and Gerry Fitt was at his country retreat in Cushendun.

On the Sunday there were two meetings in Derry. The history of one is bound into the history of the other. The first was a most emotional and war-like meeting of Sinn Fein (Kevin Street) which hardly bothered to conceal the fact that it was an open, public meeting of supporters and spokesmen of the Provisionals. By any standards the speeches were fierce. Mrs Maire Drumm, who was later to get a six-month prison sentence for her offering, said that by continuing to resist the British Army the people of Derry had got up off their knees. 'For Christ's sake stay up,' she pleaded. Then she went on : 'The only way you can avenge these deaths is by being organised, trained and disciplined until you can chase that cursed Army away. I would personally prefer to see all the British Army going back dead. But the people will not succeed with stones and bottles. They should come into the one organisation which will organise and train them. You should not shout "Up the IRA." You should join the IRA. The men must be organised and trained to fight so that they can go out and destroy the British Army for ever and ever.' Mrs Drumm's speech was followed in much the same vein by a Mr Walter Lynch, described as general secretary of Kevin Street Sinn Fein. He told the crowd that the only way to put Tuzo (the GOC) and his 'mad dogs' out of Ireland was through the IRA.

Lynch said the IRA was building and preparing to take the field in battle to drive the British Army out. He then went on to say that the IRA was actually in the field but his contradiction appears to be attributable to emotion and passion, not ignorance of what was happening in the Bogside. Lynch ended: 'Victory is within our grasp and it will come.' Finally Rory Brady, president of SF Kevin Street, spoke. He told the crowd in a detailed political speech: 'We want to stand together and walk together and struggle together under leadership and discipline and please God we'll finish it this time.' He asked the crowd: 'Are we going to put up with it for another ten years or more?' and when his words were greeted with shouts of 'No, No', he added: 'I'm glad to hear you say that because we are going to finish it this time. We're on the high road to freedom and what we need to do is to rock Stormont and to keep it rocking until Stormont comes down.' A few hundred yards away John Hume, and his colleagues from the party that he had managed to get to a meeting, heard the words and their message. Hume had O'Hanlon, Currie and of course Cooper. They met in the company of Labour TD Michael O'Leary from Dublin and when the question of withdrawing from Stormont came up O'Leary suggested that the vacuum this would create would be filled by the Provos unless the SDLP decided to try some alternative assembly idea. For the moment the idea was no more than a germ but the meeting decided to issue an ultimatum to the British Government: unless there was a full-scale public inquiry into the two deaths by Thursday they would withdraw from Stormont.

Devlin was contacted by 'phone about the decision and since it was only an ultimatum he agreed but insisted that if the party did withdraw they would have to broaden the basis for leaving and not just leave it because of a 'Derry thing'. Fitt in Cushendun could not be contacted. There was always a watertight system for contacting him via a local pub but either he didn't get messages, which is very unlikely, or he purposely refused to take calls – more probable – because he fought shy of decisions. Fitt has never been, and still is not, leader of the party in any real political sense. He is the figurehead whose value, particularly at Westminster, was immense in the early days of the Civil Rights movement. That value often almost undermined the SDLP since Fitt is also prone to agreeing with impressive British politicians, and his desire to maintain the *status quo* and get on with the job of politics, which is to him as amusing as it is vital and important, at several points almost ruined his party. One such occasion was coming now. During the next week Fitt saw Maudling and almost certainly agreed to try and change his party's mind on the demand for a full inquiry if soldiers were called to give evidence in public at the inquest. Maudling promised this but when the story leaked out MPs like Devlin literally went wild and restated their demand: an inquiry or nothing. An inquiry or we quit.

The next few days passed with no movement from either SDLP or authorities except for an effort from Faulkner on Wednesday night. He told them they could have real and effective participation in the North's affairs, a chance to do genuine constructive things together or 'they can have instant politics of exploiting every issue as it arises without consideration of the long-term effects'. Basically Faulkner was right. The SDLP attitude now was in marked contrast to that of only a few weeks back and they ignored the Prime Minister completely, never made a reference to him or called to him to do anything. It seemed hard on him that, because the British Army answerable to Westminster would not agree with them and because the British government would not accede to a request for an inquiry, the SDLP should decide to quit Faulkner's parliament. Despite the fact that he was Prime Minister, technically in control of the Army, he could justly have asked whether, since the SDLP wanted Westminster to have control over the Army and security, it would not have been better for Mr Fitt to threaten to quit Westminster instead. But pressures on the SDLP from many sides were great. Not that there was physical or personal intimidation. It was simply that in Derry where there had been peace there was now war. The SDLP would represent no-one if they did not try and win back the political initiative from the IRA. At a time when authority, any authority, was a filthy word in Derry, anyone who tried to remain part of the system was likely to run into serious political trouble. The party had to do something, it had to do something dramatic and it had to do it as quickly as possible. It decided on withdrawal despite the inconsistencies inherent in such a move.

However fascinating the procedures used in the end to get the SDLP out of parliament, their departure from a press conference on Friday 16 July was the most crushing blow that could be delivered to Faulkner, to his Government and to Stormont. The Stormont system had been unbalanced from its inception. It would always depend on Catholic support to have any chance of success. Earlier withdrawals by opposition parties in the past had not helped, but they were made for different reasons and in different circumstances. From the earliest days of the Civil Rights movement politics in the North as elsewhere had changed radically and what was Nationalist pique in one generation was much more serious in this context. Besides, the men involved were cleverer generally than their fathers and the SDLP had brought together under one umbrella for the first time a major section of anti-Unionist parliamentary opinion. So Stormont was in real trouble if the Catholics and their representatives decided to leave it. Like a see-saw, with an overweight at one end, the system had been kept in shaky balance for years by the occasional Unionist run to the barrel in the middle to steady things. O'Neill had been up to the centre many times. Faulkner's committee system idea was an effort to get there too. But when the weight at the other end decided to get off then the whole structure would inevitably collapse. From the day the SDLP left Stormont the whole future of the parliament, the government, and the entire system, was in serious and escalating doubt.

At the press conference on the Friday morning Gerry Fitt, returned from Cushendun and London, read the party statement. It was by far the longest and most detailed account the six MPs and one Senator had ever given of how they saw things in the North. It was a political apologia unequalled by them even in their launching press conference two years earlier. It must be judged to a degree, if not dishonest, at least politically opportunist in the extreme. But whatever its motives, it gathered together brilliantly the complex strands of anti-Unionist feeling at the time. It is worth a full quotation. It read:

'The Parliamentary party of the SDLP issued a statement earlier this week in which it demanded an impartial inquiry into the deaths of two young men in Derry resulting from British Army action and in which we made it clear that in the event of failure by the authorities to agree to our demand we would take a certain course of action. Our demand has not been met and we have therefore no alternative but to pursue the course of action that we have already outlined in our earlier statement. We will pursue that course of action. We pointed out also that we regarded our demand as a basic test of, and public questioning of, the sincerity and determination of the British government to proceed in an impartial manner towards a political solution of the problems of our community. We have arrived at this point of questioning as a result of a whole series of issues and events of which the Derry deaths were but the culmination and for us the last straw.

'These events have led to increasing doubts in our minds over a period of time about the usefulness of our role as parliamentary representatives within the present system. We have now been driven to the point when we have been faced with a clear choice: either to continue to give credibility to the system which in itself is basically unstable and from which derives the unrest that is destroying our community or take a stand in order to bring home to those in authority the need for strong political action to solve our problems and to prevent any further tragic loss of life which derives from the instability of our political institutions. The deaths in Derry were a final but important straw. If as responsible public representatives we were unable to obtain action on an issue such as this – an issue which has outraged our constituents – what role is there for us in the present parliamentary system? If British troops had shot unarmed civilians dead in a riot situation in the streets of Birmingham what would have been the reaction of the British public? Would there have been an inquiry? Human life has been seriously devalued by violent elements in our society. We find it intolerable that it should be devalued by those charged with the responsibility of solving our problems. By doing so they play straight into the hands of those same violent elements. The actions of both the British government and their Army in the Northern Ireland situation on this issue tend to confirm our increasing suspicions about the role of the Army completely in the present situation. These suspicions date from the arrival in power of the present administration.

'These suspicions are instanced by the military action in the curfew of the lower Falls a few short weeks after they came to power; instanced by the proposals for a full-time battalion or battalions of the UDR; instanced by the unquestioning acceptance of the truth of Army public statements; instanced by the admitted policy of virtual internment by using the normal legal process and instanced by the obviously decreasing political control of the military under the new British administration. Then we had the "shoot to kill on suspicion" policy announced by Mr Faulkner, a policy now confirmed despite the subsequent denials that there had been any change. Then we have the obvious and increasing lack of consultation between the British government and the Opposition leaders in marked and stark contrast to the previous administration which without prejudice to either side sought our view continually. The attitude of the present administration in Whitehall on this matter is either due to deliberate policy or to sheer carelessness, either of which is unpardonable in the serious situation in which we find ourselves.

'Is it any wonder that we feel that the role of the military has changed from being that of impartial keepers of the peace to that of shoring up and supporting a particular individual in the office of Prime Minister? Has the British government even yet faced the logic of its presence in Northern Ireland? Public memories are short but the memories of those who suffer are not. We would recall the circumstances of the intervention in August 1969 when the Army came to the streets to impose law and order and a reform programme was forced on Stormont.

'What did that intervention mean other than that the Northern Ireland system itself had failed to produce the basis for peace, justice and stability? Now, two years later, having refused to face the logic of the situation, the British government, without the slightest constitutional guarantee, asks us to believe that the chief architects of our injustice-ridden society – the Unionist party – are the people who can govern us towards a solution within the same system.

'Throughout those two years we have had legislative reform. We have made it clear repeatedly that the letter of reform is not the reality without a change of heart. Instead of a change of heart we have witnessed the steady and increasing grip of the system by right-wing forces in the north of Ireland. Two Prime Ministers have already fallen to their intransigence and intolerance and a third has shown repeated evidence of his willingness to bow the knee to their pressures culminating in a remarkable sight of a Prime Minister and half his cabinet obeying a summons from the Orange Order of which they are members to attend a meeting in Lurgan to discuss the question of Orange parades. Does the British government seriously believe there can be any real public confidence in a government which is still dominated by a secret sectarian society and does it believe that its Army can be used to back the decisions of such a government on the question of the routing of Orange parades which seriously threaten the peace and still be regarded as having an impartial role?

'All these have led us to the point of questioning the sincerity and determination of the British government to solve the problem. Indeed it would appear to us that it has no real policy beyond that of reacting to events as they happen and hoping that the problem will run away. Such an attitude amounts to one of irresponsibility and negligence, the more so because of the representations that we have made and the accuracy of our forecasts. In so far as we can detect any definite policy it would appear to be the maintenance of Stormont in its present form carrying our minimum civil rights reforms and involving the Opposition only to a point when the Unionist right-wing would not be alienated. In other words British policy is still governed as it always has been, except for a few short months in 1969, by the threat of a right-wing backlash. There can be no solution till the right-wing is confronted. The present policy such as it is has never had any chance of success and has now been totally shattered by our decision to withdraw from the present parliamentary system and set up an alternative assembly. By so doing we will bring home to the world the reality of the

Northern Ireland situation which is that Stormont is, and always has been, the voice of Unionism. The assembly that we propose will be the voice of non-Unionists. There can be no solution which does not take account of both and it would be our hope for this community that such account is taken sooner rather than later. There are those who will say that our attitude is neither responsible nor constructive.

'We would draw their attention to our record which has been one of constructive parliamentary and public activity against an increasingly difficult background. We have constantly condemned violence and have continually urged restraint often at political cost to ourselves and in unpopular circumstances. We now take this stand in order to bring home to those in authority in London the need for political solutions to end the instability which leads to continuing unrest here. Even the GOC points out the need for a political solution. How long must we wait? Let us make it clear once again that we deplore and condemn outright violence as a means to political ends. Those who deliberately organise and perpetrate violence in our society are only leading the people to destruction and the only ones to suffer to date, and they have suffered grievously, are those people in the areas where violence has taken place. Violent men must also take their share of responsibility for the suffering and death that results from their actions. When the first stone is thrown or the first shot fired no-one knows where it will end but anyone knowingly starting or creating a violent situation must bear his share of responsibility for the consequences. To our supporters we say firmly and clearly: stay off the streets and give no support whatever to the violence or the perpetration of it. We are determined to create a solution to this problem but violence apart from the suffering and death that it causes can only hinder us. One year ago the whole world supported our cause. This is not so today because of violence and violent men. We have heard recently the publicly expressed views of some of those who advocate violence. Does anyone really believe that we can build a decent society on such attitudes?

'Finally, may we say that we welcome the support given to our stand by our parliamentary colleagues and other groups. We withhold further details about the nature of the alternative assembly that we propose until we have had, in courtesy, the opportunity of discussing our ideas with those of our parliamentary colleagues at Stormont who have expressed support for our stand. We have also received expressions of support both public and private from local councillors and we shall seek an early meeting with all of them as well to consult with them before announcing our final detailed plan for the alternative assembly.'

So that was that. Whatever about the glaring inconsistencies which emerged when the statement was compared to what the party's attitude had been only weeks before, the main group of parliamentary Opposition MPs, with support by now from the Nationalist party and all but one other MP at Stormont, Mr Vivian Simpson, the Labour member for Oldpark, was leaving the parliamentary set-up. The situation was bound to deteriorate from now on. And a hint of what was to come was given the following Sunday when the hard-line Junior Home Affairs Minister John Taylor spoke on an RTE lunchtime radio programme. He was asked about the IRA and said: 'The IRA is growing in strength and organisation and firm action is required over the next few months to bring its activities to a prompt end. In fact if this did not materialise I myself would find it difficult to continue in government. As for the shooting in Derry – it may be necessary for the security forces to take an even firmer line with rioters. I would defend without hesitation the action taken by the Army authorities in Derry against subversives during the past week or so when it was necessary in the end to actually shoot to kill. I feel that it may be necessary to shoot even more in the forthcoming months in Northern Ireland.'

Within minutes of Taylor's comments SDLP MPs had called for his resignation. War was declared on all sides, and no time was being lost in getting the battle lines drawn.

4 INTERNMENT

The security situation had deteriorated since the beginning of 1971. By the end of July tables of deaths, both of civilians and members of the security forces, and of explosions added up to an overall picture of devastating proportions. And there were countless minor incidents every day and night which received scant attention but which kept nerves on edge in Belfast, Derry and other centres. The worst incident of the year up to the shootings of Cusack and Beattie had been the murders of the three Scottish soldiers but, although there were days, sometimes weeks, of relative if uneasy peace, each month had its share of incidents of one kind and another. As August came in the Faulkner government was only days away from introducing the policy of internment without trial. Figures like these were used to confirm the escalating security crisis:

		DEATHS		
MONTH	NO. OF EXPLOSIONS	RUC	ARMY	CIVS
Jan.	12	0	0	3
Feb.	28	2	3	6
Mar.	33	0	3	2
April	37	0	0	0
May	47	0	2	2
June	50	0	0	0
July	91	0	2	2

Before 1 August, therefore, there had been 27 civilian, police and Army deaths and a total of 298 explosions. In view of what was to follow the figures may be small but considering that nothing like this total had been recorded for 40 years its impact was bound to be immense.

There were other incidents on the security front too, which, while not in themselves of major importance, displayed such nerve that no government or security force could have turned a blind eye to them. In mid-July members of the Provisional IRA rescued a wounded volunteer from the Royal Victoria Hospital where he was receiving treatment by walking in through the main gate, holding the staff at gunpoint and calmly walking out with their colleague. He and his releasers were never captured. The next day armed Provisionals held the staff of the huge *Daily Mirror* newspaper plant at Suffolk outside Belfast at gunpoint, planted massive bombs and drove off. They wrecked the plant causing £2 million worth of damage; it was damaged beyond repair and was never re-opened by the *Mirror*. Such incidents lowered the morale of the security forces, further infuriated Faulkner and his cabinet, particularly men like Taylor who were now openly canvassing for internment, and added to growing Protestant demands for some action. By mid-July there was open discussion on the pros and cons of internment, and by the last week in the month there were persistent rumours that it would be introduced. Faulkner has always said that its purpose was to nip in the bud some massive IRA offensive which the security forces could see on the horizon: because of the gradual escalation of violence in the first eight months of the year and intelligence about the impending assault something had to be done and done quickly. And the policy of interning or detaining IRA suspects without trial or without preferring charges against them was decided upon.

When political discussion revolves around the factors which were instrumental in the eventual downfall of the government and parliament at Stormont, the question of internment emerges as one of the most vital. It was not just its military failure that was important – (indeed at other times and in different circumstances the military success of the policy might have mattered less than its deterrent value) – quite simply, the massive reaction of the entire Catholic community in Northern Ireland, combined with internment's intrinsic failures on the ground, delivered to the entire Stormont system a death-blow from which it was never to recover. If, by the introduction of internment, Faulkner had tried to cut off a threat to the state and its government and parliament he had failed totally; in fact, he had hastened the death of the very system which supported these things. And even despite the rising tide of violence, Faulkner should surely have been able, if he were indeed the astute politician he had so often been dubbed, to spot the changed situation that existed in Northern Ireland in the late summer of last year.

There were four vital reasons why internment could not work: (1) The changed nature of the IRA, the body which would provide the internees; (2) poor intelligence; (3) the attitude in the Republic and (4) the potential among the Catholic population at every level to resist.

Because it is the least important, poor intelligence can be considered first. While the B Specials were still in existence and the IRA had been essentially a rural phenomenon as it was earlier in the history of the state and again in the late fifties and early sixties, the type of localised information which the individual B man could get was vital to internment policies. B men worked in units close to their homes and the localised knowledge they had of Republicans helped greatly when rounding-up IRA sympathisers was announced as government policy. The Specials had a minor role in the cities, and in any case the IRA had not operated in the cities, hardly even in major towns.

Now in August 1971 there were no Specials and even though the IRA still operated in the country the new force that had been put in the B men's place, the UDR, was unsuited to implement the internment policy. True, there were ex-Specials in the force, but they were now under British Army control. Previously they had been under police control and had worked at genuine grassroots levels. Now they were operating in 'foreign' areas, sometimes twenty or more miles from home – twenty or more miles, in other words, from the local Republicans they knew, the local cross-border escape routes, the local

IRA men. Thus the chances of getting at that part of the IRA which operated in the country were lessened by the absence of the Specials. The British Army had no time to learn the old tricks. Nor, apparently, had they time to appreciate fully the changed nature of the IRA.

In the past the IRA, broadly-speaking, had been a smaller group of men, attempting by violence to impose a political ideal on a people which was in the main apathetic if not openly hostile. When it left the fields and the bridges it was to attack targets in towns rather than cities, and to mount operations against military and police targets, not commercial, industrial or civilian holdings. The command structure in this smaller organisation was closely-knit and more easily defined than its counter-part in the early seventies. The new IRA was different in one more – perhaps the most important – aspect : its relation to the Catholic population. As has been pointed out the idea of defending Catholics had not been an IRA function in the past, and it had been a rural organisation. But in the late sixties and early seventies this was totally changed. The IRA quite simply grew out of the sectarian rioting in August 1969 in Belfast, was given increased impetus by events like the Falls curfew and grew in strength firstly in opposition to British Army excesses like unexplained deaths and brutalities against the civilian population and finally as a result of internment itself. Whereas in the earlier days it had tried to graft itself into the population, this time it had grown straight out of the community. And when it was attacked the Catholic population would militarily have to be discomforted and would in their hearts feel – and see – the Army as acting not just against 'terrorists' but against them in toto.

Now that the IRA was an urban rather than a rural organisation, the escape routes would be the alleyways and backstreets of the Falls, the Clonard, the other Catholic ghettoes – streets in which the Army would have little chance of finding their way, especially in the dark, under pressure and when the locals had changed or taken down the street signs. So that while the rural – and smaller –

section of the IRA operating in border towns had the escape route across to the Republic – one it didn't have before because there had been internment in the South at the same time as in the North – the urban IRA had an infinitely better way of escaping the Army : the bolt-hole was a ghetto, not open country. And even today, nearly a year after internment, the IRA can still bomb and fire and escape into 'free' areas of Derry and Belfast.

The attitude in the South to the introduction of internment in the North was obviously vital. When it was last implemented the policy got co-operation from de Valera who locked up his quota of IRA men, thereby closing the cross-border escape routes. Allied with the lack of enthusiasm of the people this helped the anti-IRA drive in the North. But in 1971 it was unthinkable that Lynch should intern Republicans in the Republic. If he had of course things would have been different. If he did it today the situation would change overnight and the Provos would certainly not last long.

But by August 1971, even if the feeling in the Republic which followed the sectarian rioting of 1969 had died down to some extent, the reactions being generated daily by stories of Army brutality and events like the killing of Cusack and Beattie in Derry left Lynch and his government in no position to move politically against the openly-operating IRA. The final political nail in this coffin was of course the decision of the SDLP to withdraw from the Stormont parliament. For if the main body of anti-Unionist opinion in the North was so disaffected with the system as to get out of it, no Dublin Taoiseach could offer help to that system when it derogated from the normal processes of the law. When internment finally did come it was interesting to note that Mr Lynch condemned not the policy itself but the policies which led to its use. And whatever hopes Faulkner might have had that if internment worked in the North and met with only minor opposition Lynch would move in the South were finally dashed when internment was greeted with massive and overwhelming opposition in the North after 9 August.

Finally there was the potential among the Catholic people to resist. Reform had meant little and what little it had meant had been already further diluted after the Conservative government came to power and Brian Faulkner became Premier in Stormont. There were no new jobs, no more money in the pockets in Ballymurphy or Turf Lodge, no sense that the Catholic people were beginning to belong to the system. In other words not much had changed. For Catholics in the ghettoes, things in mid-1971 were as they had been in 1968 : wretched.

Thus the population in the areas where internment would be introduced had absolutely no incentive to be restrained or understanding of authority. And it was not just the ghettoes that would react. For a few months after August 1969 every middle-class Catholic felt things had changed and even in June 1971 they had Hume's speech in the Commons to confirm them in that view. Since social and economic matters intruded less on the lawyers, the doctors or the managers they could point to the so-called reforms as good in themselves and as offering a hope for better things in the future. Catholics who never openly opposed, say, the B men, because they were rarely their victims but who nevertheless disliked the idea of the Unionists having their own army would appreciate the advantage to society of the abolition of that force. In other words after you left the ghettoes you could still find in June 1971 middle-class Catholics still willing to give the system the benefit of the doubt and an endless set of chances. They were, after all, hardly worse off as a result of the two violent years which had passed. But events like the Derry deaths did shake a lot of middle-class folk from their lethargy. There was a stirring, a feeling that this certainly was not right and that it should have been at least inquired into. The middle-class Catholic confidence in British justice was called into question. On other points too the middle and even upper classes were being drawn into the battle : middle-class friends of the Humes, the Curries and the Coopers would hear from the MPs their sorry case stories. Lawyers and solicitors were getting more sordid riot cases particularly from the notorious Criminal Justice (Temporary Provisions) Act.

Teachers in Catholic schools were by the end of July at their wit's end to know how to answer the parents of young schoolchildren who had fallen victim to the rough-handling tactics of the Army; priests were becoming daily more involved in cases of social welfare and distress as juvenile after juvenile, youth after youth appeared to be charged, convicted and then sentenced to six months on the evidence of British soldiers – evidence which was often found to be extremely suspect. In short a wider section of the Catholic community than ever before was mentally geared to react against the further incursions which would inevitably be made if internment were introduced. The combination of those four points – poor intelligence, the changed nature and role of the IRA, the attitude in the South, and most vitally for the future of parliamentary democracy, potential opposition among the widest possible cross-section of the Catholic community, had they been studied well enough and long enough, should have been sufficient to make any politician fight shy of using the last throw in the Special Powers Act.

By the end of July, however, Faulkner had decided that there was no alternative. He had full cabinet backing even from the so-called moderates: Robin Bailie, his Commerce Minister, had even advocated the measure as a back-bencher under Chichester-Clark, and some of his hardliners like Captain Robert Mitchell favoured all manner of extraordinary ideas like flame-throwers, deportation and perpetual use of lead rather than rubber bullets. There would be no problems in the Unionist party either, at grassroots level.

With many gut Unionists the actual locking-up of Republicans has mattered less than the fact that this operation can be carried out and that the whole operation can be identified as part of an overall 'defence of the realm'. Some Unionists in Northern Ireland, obsessed with their own view of themselves as British, have, with the added advantage of the 'land frontier', tended to see themselves as somewhat of a fifth column in defending the Queen, the Kingdom and the Commonwealth. From this mentality, as much as from anti-Roman Catholic feeling, are born the 'No Surrender' and 'Not an Inch' attitudes. And into this scheme of things internment fits perfectly. I have even heard Unionists argue from the particular case of their own use of the measure to the general case of justification for it in other parts of the world at different times, made by political theorists. If it could be introduced by the British during the Second World War then it must be easily justifiable by Unionists against the IRA. Or so goes part of the argument. Internment then would meet with no really strong opposition inside the Unionist party system. Indeed while under Chichester-Clark it might have been seen as a desperate measure and not accorded a general welcome, under the guise of Brian Faulkner it would be presented as a measure reluctantly introduced, aimed at eliminating the gunmen and nothing more, and one which demanded full support. Few Unionists would bother to contemplate internment as a political issue and even months after its introduction some MPs were still trying to make the case that it hadn't anything at all to do with politics.

In the last week in July incidents increased all over the North. There were shootings nightly and even daily in Belfast and Derry particularly and a regular nightly scene in Catholic areas of the city of Belfast was one of almost total black-out, with cautious army foot patrols, some sniping or nail-bombing from the darkened shadows and a picture of tension and unease overall. On 23 July hundreds of troops took part in early morning 'dawn swoops' on the homes of Republicans. About 110 men were taken in for questioning and many thought it was internment. Most had, strangely enough, been Official Republican/IRA sympathisers and all but two men were released within hours. The two were charged with trifling offences such as possession of documents relating to an illegal organisation – the RUC special branch chestnut for keeping tabs on a Republican. Areas in Belfast such as Ballymurphy, Andersonstown, Falls, Finaghy, Stranmillis, Springfield, Smithfield, Whiterock, the Markets, and Unity Flats/New Lodge Road were combed by soldiers, while outside the city towns covered included Newry, Lurgan, Strabane, Portadown, Coalisland and other centres. Ivan Cooper commented : 'This is virtual internment. If it continues people will be back on the streets protesting very quickly.' It wasn't internment, but it was part of the plan for it.

Broadly speaking these raids were to improve intelligence for the internment operation. The mind boggles at the thought of the former B Specials embarking on such raids before taking part in the actual operation, but the plain fact is that the non-Irish security forces needed such a 'dummy run' to give them any chance on the night. On Tuesday 27 July, much to Faulkner's surprise, Lynch in the Republic ordered raids on homes of Sinn Fein members too. Several prominent Republicans had their papers rifled by plain clothes special branch men and there were men held too for 'further questioning'. All the operations were done under the Offences Against the State Act, a piece of legislation almost as odious to Republicans and their supporters as the Special Powers Act. Rumours that the Dublin raids meant Lynch was willing and ready to co-operate if Faulkner turned for internment were rife in Belfast. Rumours also continued to circulate to the effect that Faulkner was daily pressing for the operation but that Reginald Maudling was opposed to it.

Maudling decided to correct this tale on a television programme. On Wednesday 28 July he told the Tory backbench Home Affairs committee that he was not against internment, that he was not in any way whatever 'holding the introduction of it up' and he added : 'We shall not shrink from introducing it if necessary.' The language of a man who knows what he is talking about and knows that it is not far off.

On 1 August there were more raids on Republican homes in Belfast. The night before, following his speech to backbenchers, Maudling had been interviewed on Ulster

Television, and said that if internment were to be introduced there would be no advance warning. The second dummy run was enough for most IRA men. If internment wasn't coming something else was, and if they couldn't describe it they could feel it and they didn't like it. Contingency plans of all sorts were laid in great detail for senior Provisionals and the Official IRA made its preparations. As the second session of raids ended the Civil Rights Association met in Belfast and, with 300 people present, also agreed to make internment contingency plans. These were begun immediately and it was mooted that even civil rights workers and left-wingers, in no way at all connected with violence, might be lifted too if the Stormont regime decided to move against all opposition forces within the state. In Catholic ghettoes and even in housing estates like Andersonstown which were far from being ghettoes there was a feeling of preparedness. The Provisionals there were certain that internment was coming. In many ways it would play into their hands.

On Tuesday 3 August the cabinet met at Stormont and waffled about the need for abiding by whatever the security forces would have to say on internment. But basically the ministers around Faulkner now accepted the idea and were resigned to the fact that the last available throw was about to be given to the dice. Faced with the escalating security situation a Unionist Prime Minister used to have two choices, neither of which of course excluded the other: he could call out the Specials or he could intern. In fact those two choices represented the only real, tangible expression of power available to a Stormont government. Control over internal security is the only power in Northern Ireland. With no Specials to summon to the aid of the state now, internment through the Special Powers Act was Faulkner's last card. On Thursday 5 August the security unit met at Stormont and Army and RUC chiefs were present. After the meeting Faulkner and Tuzo went to London where the final details of the operation, now agreed upon, were thrashed out. These details were not those which would be followed out in the end.

In fact it was agreed that internment would be introduced on 10 August. All Belfast, Derry and other centre-units of the Army were advised of this and sat back to wait. Among the security boffins at Stormont Castle there was the hope that perhaps when it came the IRA would think that the internment swoop was yet another trial run and thus that reaction to it would be lessened. On Saturday 7 August Harry Thornton, a Newry worker, was driving past Springfield Road RUC station when his car back-fired. A soldier in the post who thought the sound was a shot ran into the road and opened fire. Thornton was shot dead. As soldiers followed up and reached the car, which was stopped at traffic lights at the junction of the Falls and Springfield Roads, Thornton's mate got out and ran round to his friend who was slumped over the driving wheel. He was brutally attacked by soldiers, taken to Springfield Road station and later beaten up. As the soldiers were gathering round, local people testify that some were gleeful: 'We got one, we got one,' they shouted. Harry Thornton's death was carried out erroneously by a soldier acting under the type of order which the Prime Minister had been politically pilloried for weeks earlier.

For hours after this killing the Clonard area went wild. Thornton was unknown, not from the area, a nobody. But word of his murder spread and people poured on to the streets to show their anger: women lit candles at a make-shift shrine, youths threw stones, petrol bombs and whatever they could lay hands on. The Provisionals waited until dark and engaged the Army. The trouble was fierce but no more fatalities occurred and by Sunday an uneasy peace of sorts had descended on Catholic areas again. As midnight came on the Sunday the order went out from Army HQ at Lisburn that the operation of internment had been brought forward 24 hours. Shortly before 1 a.m. British soldiers began to leave their posts, join mobile units and patrols and head off into the darkened streets and side-streets of Belfast, Derry, Newry, Strabane and other centres. Internment was about to begin.

The main point about internment is not that it failed militarily, since this is so self-evident as to be hardly worth underlining. What is important about it in 1971 is the way in which the entire Catholic population became united against it. To this day not one single Catholic individual or association, organisation or group, let alone member of political party or parliament, has lent his voice to internment, with the possible exception of Dr G. B. Newe who had joined Mr Faulkner's cabinet in late 1971 and might therefore be said to have acquiesced in retrospect in the decision. In fact he disagreed with it completely and never discussed it except to oppose it within the cabinet room. If internment was a military catastrophe and a source of recruitment for the Provisionals it was more vitally the single great issue which united Catholics against the Stormont government, parliament and whole system. Nothing in the history of Stormont had done so much to bring the Catholic community together. Never had they been so united on any issue. Never had the combined weight of more than 34 per cent of the North's population turned its face so forcefully against any measure. And by that measure stood or fell Mr Faulkner and his administration, Stormont and its parliament. So that, as internment was maintained, Catholic opposition to it grew. And as Catholic opposition grew it became even more certain that the SDLP, for example, would not go back to Stormont, that hitherto uncommitted sections of the Catholic population were now so alienated from the system that they would never again recognise it, and that the cumulative effect of all these factors would ensure that Stormont was daily and nightly being dealt a series of blows from which it could not recover.

The bald statistics of the first few days of internment must surely have made Westminster politicians wonder whether they had been sold a pup by the tenacious Faulkner. The crude politicking which had banned the Apprentice Boys parade at the same time as announcing internment was shown up for what it was when even Protestants like Ian Paisley and Desmond Boal pointed to the two measures as having been introduced for political rather than security reasons and as being in any event too late, weak in principle and badly implemented. Certainly this last point was a telling factor not only in the military failure of internment but in its subsequent social failure as well. Had the job been done cleanly and accurately much might have been forgiven. The fact is however that it was a ham-fisted, crude and brutal affair which disgraced the British Army, made nonsense of their so-called ability as intelligence officers, brought them into disrepute throughout the world and ended up with an official inquiry which, even though boycotted by men who had been arrested, was to find, despite its semantic quibbling, that nearly everyone arrested had been 'ill-treated' by security forces. The public relations effect of the mis-management of internment was the final straw for the policy. Every single piece of publicity issued after it was bad for the government. As the death toll mounted, Catholics 'dropped out' of Northern society, and released detainees told of their treatment, it became clear that the policy was a disaster.

What followed internment, militarily speaking, was war. What followed internment in the hearts and minds of the Catholic population was total alienation: Brian Faulkner was to speak in the days after the measure was first brought in of support among the Catholic population for it. Either that was a downright lie or the Catholics were telling him lies: for from nowhere did any Catholic emerge to support the move. As internment completed the estrangement of the Catholic population from the regime the future of Stormont became more and more of a foregone conclusion. No parliament in the world, in the unique and peculiar set of conditions which faced Stormont, would have survived anyway and this parliament, already stripped of even the facade of democracy, was even more certain to fall. It was never to get even a chance to reprieve itself despite efforts that Faulkner was to make later in the year. From the day the opposition had walked out Stormont was on the slippery slope; when soldiers began arresting men on 9 August under the Special Powers Act it became more and more a question of time before the system reached the bottom of that slope.

Bound up with the internment decision and its effect on the ground was the corresponding decision by the Catholic population to group themselves in legal and illegal opposition. In this, the strike weapon was to prove vital. If Protestants ever want to bring Northern Ireland to its knees all they need do is strike. This was to be demonstrated in Belfast and other centres for example when the Vanguard movement protested against direct rule a few days after it came. For Catholics after internment there was no such easy choice. There is no factory or workplace in Belfast for example so loaded with Catholic employees that it could close completely and those places where Catholics might be in the majority would not be sufficiently vital to cause serious disruption. In some of the building and allied industries Catholics are employed heavily but these jobs would not necessarily hit industry or paralyse the community at once: their effect would take weeks, maybe months, to be seen since such industries have a high running raw material ratio and the availability of alternative jobs to keep the remaining staff employed if one section walked out. There are no shipyards, aircraft factories or engineering works where the Catholic minority can exercise their power by withdrawal of labour. So, after internment, some new way of exercising protest had to be found.

In retrospect it now seems so logical that it is surprising it should have taken even a few days to think of it or put it into action: Catholics would strike, not against management or commerce, but against the state. If they could not exactly picket a political system they would do the next best thing by withholding payment, absenting from councils and public authorities, leaving nominated office. The withholding of payments would be directed at local authorities to ensure that the already vexed ghetto community was even more involved. So within days of the first arrests, notices, printed at speed, were going up in windows of Catholic houses all over the North. 'Rent and

Rates Strike Here' they said. The message was simple, the effect devastating. Again, as with the military failure of internment, it was not so much the damage done to the economy by the strikes as the damage done to the whole system that mattered. What do you do when a whole section of a community decides to show its disapproval by withholding rent? Put them all in jail? There wouldn't be enough prisons for them. Take the money some other way, for example through supplementary benefits? This was what the government did and while it has recouped some of the money it is impossible to recoup the spirit that put people on rent and rate strike in the first place. Only a matter of weeks after the strike began the whole concept of paying rent, rates, local taxes of any description, even hire purchase payments, had become among the working-class and even middle-class Catholic populations an unthinkable notion. One story sums up the situation. Near Christmas a woman came into the SDLP offices in Belfast and asked to speak to Paddy Devlin. She explained that she was, of course, on rent and rate strike but she wanted to know if it would be 'all right' to get Christmas gifts in some shop by placing a deposit and putting the rest down to 'civil disobedience'. Devlin told her to do as she liked. Afterwards he said she would anyway so what was the use of trying to explain it to her? But underlying the success of the civil disobedience campaign was a failure which helped it work: that was the failure of reform in Northern Ireland as a whole.

5 THE FAILURE OF REFORM

It would probably be closer to the truth to say that real reform, reform that would have had any significance, was never tried in Northern Ireland, only thought about. From 1920, falsely created, not wanted even by the Unionists and with few friends anywhere, the Northern state had so many built-in anomalies and imbalances that in many respects it is a wonder it survived so long: fifty years is by any stretch of the imagination a long run for an experiment in government. From the beginning, of course, the greatest single problem for the government of the day would be the Catholic population: an unwilling, built-in time bomb in an essentially Protestant state. Had Catholics been in a tiny minority, they could have been ignored totally; had they been fifty per cent they would have been able to deadlock politics unless power was shared. With half the population, not even gerrymandering would hold them back and some power must have come their way. As it was however, the Catholic population, hovering in and around the thirty per cent mark was, in Unionist eyes a threat that needed to be suppressed – and probably could be – rather than a substantial community that needed to be coaxed and that would require some hand in power, even if only for its own self-respect.

But no substantial, meaningful effort was made in the early days after the foundation of the state to involve Catholics. Within weeks of the first sitting of the Northern parliament, boycotted by anti-Unionists, the vicious circle that would dominate politics North and South for fifty years had begun: unbending attitudes on one side were met with intransigence on the other. As no hand was offered from the Unionists, what could the anti-Unionists grasp in friendship? And, as the Unionists saw it, what was the point in offering the hand when it wouldn't be accepted.

The generation of men who went into Northern public life in the twenties on the Catholic/Nationalist side remembered vividly the foundation of the Northern state. They remembered for example that when the crunch came the Unionist party in Belfast had been quite prepared to 'ditch' the loyalists in three of Ulster's nine counties, never mind those further afield in the South. The boundaries of the Northern state acceptable to Unionists were those encompassing that area where, come what might, they would always have a majority. Such a set-up does not encourage co-operation among a minority community. It particularly discourages co-operation in politics: it is one thing for a man to know he cannot get on the team because he isn't good enough; it is quite another if he knows he won't make the side because the rules of the game being played preclude him in the first place.

The artificially-formed Northern state, then, had perhaps two main choices if it were to survive: it could create a system which allowed by its nature power to be shared or it could parcel out its riches in such a way that, while power wasn't shared, the powerless were at least beneficiaries of the overall system. But in fact the Unionists did neither. They took to themselves everything: government, parliament, control. Control even where the Catholics were in a majority as in Derry and Fermanagh. From the start the by-words were those of the Orangeman: 'No Surrender', 'Not an Inch', 'This we Will Maintain'. A Catholic, quite simply, while he might not have been beaten about the head by his Protestant countrymen whenever they met, counted for absolutely nothing in the new Northern state.

In a recent United Nations Association pamphlet on Northern Ireland, Professor Harry Calvert of the University of Newcastle-upon-Tyne has put some points particularly well. He writes:

'Let me state at the outset what I believe the central issue to be. The 1920 Act establishes provincial institutions of government in Northern Ireland on the British pattern. The constitutional scheme provided (not surprisingly) for the vesting of power, in these institutions, in the majority party on the English model. Because of continuing insecurity on the constitutional question and pure sectarianism, parties have continued to split on sectarian lines. The majority has always been the Unionist, Protestant, party linked with the Orange Order and to some extent a closed association. It, therefore, has always wielded power in these institutions of government; i.e. it has had a majority of members in the House of the Northern Ireland parliament, it has formed the government of Northern Ireland in which all power is vested. Looking at the obverse side what this means is that, politically, the Roman Catholic in Northern Ireland counts for virtually nothing. It matters not how able he is, how dedicated he is, even how loyal he is. The government does not need the support of Catholic members of parliament. Unionist members of parliament normally do not need Roman Catholic votes. The Roman Catholic community has literally nothing to bargain with politically. And, politically, he who cannot bargain gets a very poor deal.

'I have stated what I feel to be the basic issue because it is rather different from what has been voiced as the basic issue.

'The continued demand of recent years has been for civil rights. It is true that in some respects Roman Catholics have had reason to complain about their legal status. Thus, a local government franchise biased in favour of property interests tended to disfavour the unpropertied Roman Catholic section of the community and public powers in the fields of housing and employment have been used to discriminate. But, by and large, the disabilities of Roman Catholics were not such as to vindicate the turmoil now besetting the province. They were symptoms of the disease rather than the disease itself. Legally speaking, Roman Catholics always had full franchise rights so far as the Northern Ireland parliament was concerned, and there has been voiced no legal grievance which could not have been put right by that body – so that all the Roman Catholic community needed to do was elect the parliament it wanted and pass the reforming legislation.

'Thus stated, it is obvious that the problem is not so much one of legal as one of social and political status and power. The problem is not how to make Roman Catholic participation in the running of the state legally permissible but factually possible. It has not, however, always been voiced in these terms. Indeed, it seems rarely to have been understood in these terms until relatively recently.

'Not unnaturally, much of the early concern was not so much with the problem of exclusion from participation but with its consequences, particularly in so far as a consequence was abuse of legislative and administrative power due to lack of effective control over the exercise of such power.'

If I read him correctly, then, it would be hard to disagree except perhaps on occasional minor points, with Professor Calvert's thesis that the real problem in Northern Ireland has always been power and its possession. Protestants have had it until March of 1972, Catholics, with rare and generally insignificant exceptions, have never had a look in. Thus the reaction to the direct rule move of the British government was predictable and natural. For Protestants and Unionists were deprived of power, and Catholics, while not given that power, were at least to see that Protestants, as political animals were reduced to their status:—for the first time. Now, in Northern Ireland, with a Secretary of State ruling the state from Westminster with complete power, Protestant and Catholic are as near equal in the eyes of 'government' as they can be. Mr Faulkner's word demonstrably counts for no more with Mr Whitelaw than does the word of, say, John Hume or other anti-Unionist politicians.

In Northern Ireland there was never a real approach made to talk to Catholics until the latter days of the Premiership of Lord O'Neill. Under Sir James Craig, John Andrews, and particularly under Lord Brookeborough, the North stood still, or lurched forward a few steps behind Britain while staring sullenly as the Free State in the South, through de Valera and others sold the message of unification but did nothing about it practically. Reform was never politically mentioned until the late sixties. And then its beginnings were tentative.

It was only in October 1968 that the frail notion of reform in Northern Ireland began to see the light of day following the growth of the civil rights movement. What had begun with little fuss, when Austin Currie squatted in a house in Caledon, Co. Tyrone, because it had been allocated to an unmarried Protestant girl while Catholic families were left on the housing list, had mushroomed into the famous 5 October march in Derry which was attacked by police and which drew the attention of the world to Northern Ireland. As a result of Derry, O'Neill and two Ministers, Craig who was then at Home Affairs and Faulkner in charge of Commerce, went to London to meet the then British Prime Minister, Harold Wilson, and his Ministers. The talks concentrated on the situation in Derry, local government voting rights, housing allocations, the Special Powers Act, security generally and the idea of an ombudsman for the North. It took more than a fortnight, during which time there were more marches and some rioting in Derry, for the Unionist government and parliamentary party to agree on the North's first real reform programme.

But the programme satisfied no one. It was : (1) Housing : local authorities would be required in future to allocate houses on the basis of an agreed scheme such as a points system; (2) Central government would get an ombudsman; (3) A development commission would be appointed for Derry; (4) Consideration would be given to a review of the local government franchise but only when the government had decided the basis for overall local government restructuring; and (5) the Special Powers Act – the parts of it which conflicted with international standards would be withdrawn 'as soon as the Northern Ireland government considers this can be done without hazard'.

The abolition of the gerrymandered Derry council and its replacement by a commission was a good step forward particularly for the city itself since the chances of progress or any development under the Unionist-run council, dominated by its Mayor, Commander Albert Anderson, were negligible. But there was nothing in the other parts of the programme which went anywhere near civil rights demands on the franchise for complete 'one man, one vote'. But it was a beginning. From that date support began to flood in for O'Neill, people signed their names to letters to the newspapers and forms were printed in the *Belfast Telegraph* which people could circulate and sign in larger numbers. By December, mainly because of headline speeches by William Craig, O'Neill was going on television to the nation beginning . . . 'Ulster stands at the cross-roads' and ending 'what kind of Ulster do you want?' both phrases which were to ring around the North then, and even now be quoted from time to time.

More response came to him for this speech and the rise of the moderates began in Northern Ireland. With it began the rise of the extremists and there was little doubt who would win. It has always been easier in Northern Ireland to be an activist, an aggressor, a street politician than it has been to be a calming, moderating influence. When passions run so high, the man who shouts 'Fire' is listened to and obeyed quicker than the man who calls 'Hold'. It is the nature of politics in the North. O'Neill now sacked Craig and got a vote of confidence by 28 to 4 from his parliamentary party. But civil rights demands continued and O'Neill's position became precarious.

From that date O'Neill knew his friends and his enemies pretty clearly and he had two alternatives: woo his enemies or call his friends to help him in a general election. He choose the latter course eventually in February after losing Faulkner, William Morgan, his Minister of Health and Social Services and Mr Joe Burns, who was a junior whip. In the election, a fact that seems often to have been forgotten, O'Neill actually won: that is to say that a majority of MPs returned to parliament supported him. But the election was more vital for another reason in that it saw returned to Stormont new young MPs who had been associated with the civil rights movement: the names of John Hume, Paddy Devlin, Ivan Cooper, Paddy O'Hanlon and Paddy Kennedy were well-known at marches for months. Now they were in Stormont in most cases at the expense of the Nationalist party which had

76

been swept aside in the excitement of the civil rights movement.

O'Neill of course suffered a blow to his prestige when only being returned on a minority vote against Ian Paisley and the People's Democracy leader, Michael Farrell. Immediately after the election Unionist MPs gave O'Neill a vote of confidence. But there followed explosions at vital installations, almost certainly caused by Protestant extremists, political toing and froing and eventually in late April O'Neill resigned and Chichester-Clark took over, winning by a single vote from Faulkner. The first tentative efforts at reform had been tried but apart from the Derry commission idea it had taken a long time to get the Unionist party to accept 'one man one vote'. Only on 9 May, did the party's ruling standing committee accept the principle. Earlier the cabinet and the parliamentary party had agreed, the latter group by 28 to 22 votes.

But by far the most significant point in discussing the whole question of reform and attempted change in Northern Ireland is in the period from late August 1969 to October-November of the same year. This period is of vital significance in the history of how Stormont eventually fell, for if events then had taken a different turn the final downfall could at least have been put off for generations and at best might have come under different and less tense and strained circumstances.

Broadly speaking what happened after the August 1969 rioting in which ten people died, was that the British Labour government saw the need for quick and effective short-term answers which, while hopefully not completely alienating the Protestants upon whom the Stormont government of the day depended, would at the same time reassure Catholics who distrusted the security forces and the Unionist government, and reaffirm that they had a right to a part in the administration at least of Northern Ireland.

In October 1969, a committee under Lord Hunt reported on the reorganisation of the local security forces, the RUC and the Ulster Special Constabulary. It recommended that the Specials be disbanded and the police disarmed. It was in the eyes of Catholics an almost unbelievable reform: at one stroke the most hated and distrusted section of the Administration – its private army – and its most recognisable agency was gone, while the police, against whom massive distrust had built up during the rioting in August, were now stripped of the guns which, among other things, had killed without reason at least three Catholic civilians, one of them a nine-year-old boy. The Catholic reaction was one of total satisfaction right across the board. It was heightened by the fact that an independent inquiry had provided the exact result that Catholics had asked for.

The failure, however, of that very vital reform can be taken as indicative of the failure of all the others: already it has been seen that there was a total failure to patrol the barricaded Catholic areas with the reformed police service created by Hunt thus resulting in the RUC retaining their pre-October image in the eyes of Catholics. Then as time passed and events escalated, the police were gradually re-armed, the new Ulster Defence Regiment began to recruit Protestants at about six to seven times the rate of Catholics so that in Catholic eyes it became a different form of B Specials only in so far as it was under British Army not RUC control. Even this point melted away as the British Army deteriorated in Catholic eyes from a peace-keeping force to a force propping-up the Stormont government. But all the reforms brought in since the days of O'Neill, up to the traumatic weeks in October have either failed or were not worthy of the name reform in the first place. And here we have the crucial point: for if the whole idea of reform was to try and improve the existing Stormont system, make Catholics more involved with the state and try to allow them play their part, then when this plan failed not only would Catholics revert to their former position as second-class and disgruntled citizens, but they would in fact be worse off having been apparently promised something that didn't materialise with all the frustrations that this situation implies. In other words the reforms of 1969 began by infuriating the Protestant population and falsely encouraging the Catholic population. The former would harden its attitudes logically and understandably, but disastrously, while the latter would end up being disappointed and totally embittered and disillusioned.

When that happened the prospect for further initiatives to reconcile the two communities would be even more remote and the chances of survival for the parliamentary system would become increasingly slim. For as the failure of reform became more and more apparent attention focused naturally on Stormont and when Stormont was examined it was found that it couldn't reform itself and continue in existence.

Ireland, both north and south, is extremely conservative: people in trouble or in doubt, in fear or in anxiety, turn first to their parliament to effect change. When it fails, and only when it fails or is seen to be failing, do they willingly support other channels. And when that begins to happen the parliament itself loses respect, authority and most important of all support. This happened almost from the day reform was first broadcast in late 1969. It is a traceable process.

The famous Downing Street communiqué issued following discussions in London in 1969 between the British Home Secretary, James Callaghan, and the Northern government, listed the reforms which the British government had agreed to have implemented in Northern Ireland by the Stormont administration. Later communiqués after the Home Secretary had visited the north in late August and again in October re-emphasised the changes outlined in that communiqué. Those proposed changes, at least in part, might under a different system have offered genuine hope to the community in fulfilling its most important need at the time – the restoration of peace and the creation of a situation in which sectarian strife would never again break out.

To begin, then, at the beginning of the Autumn reforms of 1969. The series of reforms dealing generally with

79

security and law and order were those most widely welcomed by the Catholic community. Accordingly their failure has had the most impact. The Downing Street declaration said on the police that the principle of a civilianised and unarmed force was accepted and that an overall police authority would be set up representative of the whole community. The authority was set up by the Police Act (NI) 1970 and technically it now controls the RUC. A Public Prosecutor for the courts, to relieve police of all prosecuting duties was to be established and the Ulster Special Constabulary was to be replaced by a volunteer force under the direct control of the British Army. But what happened these reforms?

When the RUC men lost their guns after the Hunt Report there were genuine hopes that a reformed force might be able to win back confidence from the Catholic community. The Inspector-General, Mr Anthony Peacocke, resigned and was replaced by Sir Arthur Young, who was seconded from his post as Commissioner in the London Metropolitan Police. Peacocke has recently been criticised by the report of Mr Justice Scarman who investigated disturbances in Belfast and Derry as well as other centres in August 1969. With Young in the saddle and the RUC disarmed the immediate aim should have been to try and establish patrols in the barricaded areas. Young toured Derry's Bogside, for example, with Callaghan, the two of them behaving like circus comedians as they jostled their way through an October crowd.

'I've brought the new Inspector General for you. Here he is, Sir Arthur Young,' said Callaghan in the heart of the Bogside.

'God bless Sir Arthur,' the crowd shouted and the peasant in them, confronted by two Englishmen, appeared.

But apart from this outward display of the Irish inferiority complex there was a more unfortunte aspect to the whole scene. Young and Callaghan had gone in to the Bogside alone, with not another policeman in sight. It was a fatal mistake. The Bogside would take Sir Arthur and 'Sunny' Jim because they thought they saw in them the victory over the ascendancy of the Protestants. But it wouldn't be Young and Callaghan who would have to patrol the streets. The whole episode was embarrassing, as embarrassing as Young's later visits to the Falls area in Belfast where he met local residents and talked cleverly about law and order and how much he understood the fears of the Catholic population. That was one thing : the projection of an image of peace and reconciliation was a good idea. But failure to put the new, reformed, unarmed RUC into the Catholic ghettoes in October 1969 was a most disastrous policy from which the security situation never recovered. One must point clearly here that this is not a retrospective call for imposing on a frightened people a force to which they were hostile. It is simply to point out that once the initial opportunity had been lost of letting the RUC be seen to be impartial then it would never come back. That was the real failure in 1969, not the fact that it might have let the IRA form behind the barricades (which they didn't in fact do anyway), but the fact that it never gave either the police or the people a chance to accept each other. The gimmick, the publicity stunt, the political trick was chosen.

At that time too there were only two crucial areas where the RUC needed to go : the lower Falls in Belfast and the Bogside in Derry. And at that time, unlike now, the politicians like Devlin in Belfast and Hume and Cooper in Derry could have delivered the political goods. The chance was missed in late 1969. The failure, too, of the new police Authority was another underscoring of the failure of the Stormont system. In its first year the new authority should have been making itself heard and felt. It did hardly anything and what it did smacked badly of politics in so far as it never attempted to exercise its statutory control over the police. The Authority always seemed to regard the Ministry of Home Affairs as still properly in charge of the RUC. It failed lamentably in its duties and it failed from the start when it had the benefit of whatever good-will it required to get off the ground. Indeed when in August 1971 a Belfast Catholic councillor, John Flanagan, fled the city after turning up at an IRA-style press conference and it was announced that he was 'a member of the police Authority', many of even the better-informed local journalists had to go hunting high and low to find the names of the other members or any reference to the Authority's work in the year it had been in office. The Authority itself was formed with a reasonable proportion of Catholics but its administrative staff and clerical make-up came from the Home Affairs department at Stormont where a Catholic is a rare bird indeed, particularly in any sort of responsible office. The Authority had legal power to establish an independent tribunal to consider complaints against the police. But it didn't do so. The RUC continue to handle complaints against themselves.

On a small matter like the police uniform the Authority was conspicuous by its silence. Hunt had suggested that a change of uniform might not be a bad idea and this suggestion was never turned down by the members of the force itself. But the Authority never lifted a finger to implement what would have been an important minor reform. If, for example, the RUC had been seen to be changed it could have helped enormously in Catholic areas. As for the question of arms for the police, this unfortunately became a foregone conclusion as the situation deteriorated after October 1969. No doubt the principle, that police would normally be unarmed, was good: but Hunt had made it clear that there should be a supply of arms available 'when and where necessary'. It only remained therefore for someone in authority to decide when and where arms were necessary and out they would come. And in this context it should be remembered that the only head to roll after Hunt was Peacocke's. Some of the other pre-Hunt senior officers who were just as much involved in the disasters of August 1969 not only were still in the force but were actually promoted to even higher positions. So that where the Catholic community could and did find individual police officers on the ground who were genuinely ashamed of what had happened and who were of a reforming outlook the overall pattern quickly became that of a police force reformed in the eyes of British or Stormont politicians, acceptable perhaps to the Malone Road upper-class district of Belfast where police were rarely seen anyway, but much the same in the eyes of the people who mattered most : the Catholic community in the ghettoes. An example that continues to be quoted to this day is that of the death of Patrick Rooney in Belfast.

Patrick Rooney was shot dead in his own bedroom in Divis Towers, a huge skyscraper of Catholic flats, during the August 1969 riots. Police machine-gun fire from a Shorland armoured car killed him. The men who drove and fired the shots are identifiable to the police authorities, yet despite a recent confirmation in the Scarman report of what happened, no action of any kind has ever been taken against any constable. Indeed out of the many incidents involving death, injury and loss of property over the last three years for which either the police or the B Specials were clearly responsible, whether by outright killing as in the Rooney case, or by negligence as in the case of standing-by while Protestant mobs attacked Catholic property, no police officer or B Special has ever appeared in court to answer a charge. The best the Catholic community got was from Young who, having personally set up an inquiry into how Samuel Devenny, a Derry man, had died following a beating he received from RUC men in the city, came to the conclusion that within the force there was a 'conspiracy of silence' to protect the guilty men. That was that.

Law and order powers are all that Stormont had to demonstrate its authority. When reforms were shouted abroad in those areas much was expected of them. When they failed, the system was quite properly held responsible. For always within the grip of the Stormont set-up existed the ability to reform, had the desire been there. The failure of the police reforms for several reasons and the failure of the police Authority were to prove of a most serious nature for the whole institution of Stormont.

No reform was greeted so enthusiastically by Catholics as that which disbanded the B Specials. After August 1969 and the handling of the sectarian disturbances by the RUC and the Specials, it was made clear in London that the B men as a force would soon cease to exist as they had been known. In August it had been made clear that the force, as long as it survived, was going to be put under the command of the British Army and would no longer work hand in glove with the RUC. The British government then set up a committee under Lord Hunt to study the reorganisation of local security forces. But it seems pretty clear that even before this the Specials were doomed and the committee was to advise not on their end but on how that end should be effected.

The force set up to take the place of the Specials, the UDR (already as has been noted it fell into recruitment difficulties) gained initially by virtue of its being under British Army control but this 'honeymoon' period went as soon the the Army fell into disrepute in Catholic eyes. Just as the B men and the RUC suffered from each other – whatever one force did some of the blame rubbed off on the other – so too whenever the Army would be criticised or the UDR, the effect was to create further opposition to both. The UDR itself has, as promised, been kept well away from street disturbances and its task at the moment must be one of the more difficult in Northern Ireland since it mans roadblocks and provides easier sniper targets than the more mobile and more experienced British troops.

As for the office of public prosecutor, some idea of Unionist urgency in introducing this reform can be gauged from the fact that the first incumbent, Mr Barry Shaw, Q.C., took up office only in April 1972, nearly three years after the idea was proposed.

One may talk endlessly, but this type of foot-dragging is what encourages wide sections of the Catholic community to believe that while a Stormont government can introduce repressive legislation in a late-night sitting, it takes years to get a reform even onto the statute books. In this case the sluggishness was all the more regrettable because as rioting went on and such measures as the Criminal

Justice (Temporary Provisions) Act (NI) came into being, the job of prosecuting became a delicate one indeed. That Act provided for mandatory six month sentences for those found guilty of riotous behaviour and it was of course left to the discretion of police prosecutors as to whether they would charge a man with riotous behaviour if he was arrested in a street incident or with the lesser charge of disorderly behaviour which did not incur the mandatory penalty. As riots occurred in both Catholic and Protestant areas in 1970 and again in 1971 there were continual charges from local Catholic representatives and lawyers that young men from Catholic areas were being charged with riotous behaviour while their Protestant counterparts were being charged with the lesser offence. This allegation, be it said, was strenuously denied in the House of Commons at Stormont by the Attorney-General, Mr Basil Kelly, but the idea that it was operative in practice lingered among the Catholic community. Line upon line of Catholic youth in the Belfast and Derry courts did little to offset the impression that justice was being partially doled out. Thus what began as a lack of confidence in police on the ground due to a failure of reforms to be seen effective, was spreading to other areas of the administration of the law.

The final promise of reform in the security field was a crucial one since it involved the sensitive Special Powers Act. As far back as 1968 O'Neill's government, as has been seen, promised to withdraw those sections of the Act which were out of line with international standards in the field of civil rights and civil liberties. No specific mention of the act was made in the reform packages as such in the autumn of 1969 but it was made clear that the Act was regularly discussed and considered. It remains *in toto* on the statute book at this moment and of course has always been the vital act for a Unionist government since it embodies the ability to intern men without trial and to exercise other repressive measures against any section or sections of the community. There cannot be much doubt that the simple reason for the refusal of the Stormont government to make any move on the Act was because no such government would willingly give away the powers inherent in the Act. Thus whatever hope the minority community may have had that a move might be made on removing this Act, these were in the first place misunderstood and misplaced due to ignorance and when nothing materialised it added to the conviction that Stormont did not wish to reform either itself or Northern society as a whole.

A second and potentially important, though by no means vital, area of reform was in the twin fields of local and central government administration. A good while before the 1969 Downing Street communiqué the Stormont government had itself set up the office of Parliamentary Commissioner for Complaints. Basically this office was to investigate complaints of discrimination against central government. Its first occupant was the British ombudsman, Sir Edmund Compton. The second stage was a similar office for local government and this was a firm commitment in the August 1969 communiqué. The Act bringing this office into existence was quickly passed and the North, from the autumn of 1969 onwards, had two men looking into allegations against authorities. Modelled on the British system which was designed to deal with bureaucratic excesses and discrepancies, it couldn't possibly cope with the Northern situation where the whole point of discrimination was that those practising it were especially careful not to make the type of mistake that could be identified as sectarian. In other words, no manager offering a job would be stupid enough to say, never mind write, that he was refusing an applicant because of his religion. In Northern Ireland you don't have to declare your hand in this matter. If the people cannot exactly tell by sight – and many of them would claim this ability – then such things as Christian names particularly (surnames can be doubtful), schools attended, membership of clubs and most importantly place of residence rapidly identify a man beyond doubt. There isn't a system devised yet by man that can penetrate the mind and heart of a boss refusing a worker a job for one reason and stating quite plainly that it is for another. This type of situation, for example, that should have been investigated by either or both of these two officers could be found in Belfast and Fermanagh.

In East Belfast the Harland and Wolff shipyards employ roughly 10,000 men of whom only about 500 are Catholic. The spurious answer given privately to this scandalous state of affairs is that the hinterland for the labour force is almost 90 per cent Protestant although there is the small Catholic enclave of Seaforde and adjoining streets not far away. But even if this excuse were accepted it would place another large firm in West Belfast in some difficulties. This is the large engineering works of James Mackie on the Springfield Road. It is literally surrounded on all sides by Catholic houses, yet the number of employees from that religion working there can be counted, 'on the fingers of one hand'. True there is a Protestant area a few hundred yards up the Springfield Road but it seems strange at least that this firm never managed to draw a labour pool from the Falls, Clonard, Broadway or Springfield Road areas all of which are Catholic enclaves. These cases are typical of the North's discrimination which is in-built and deep-seated.

Somehow the false impression got across that reform would mean something to this situation, that change would mean change in the factories or on the ground, that it would be recognisable. Alas the reality turned out to be far from satisfactory. Catholics had no more chance of employment after reform than they had before. Reform might have been an acceptable middle-class concept in some areas though even this wore off quickly, but it didn't create one extra job or put one extra penny in a pocket, particularly a Catholic pocket.

In investigating local authority behaviour in the North the Cameron Commission had already found more than enough to justify the expressions of protest that had been made since the start of the civil rights movement and now, it was believed, a machinery was being set up to investigate the contemporary scene and look at running complaints on a day-to-day basis. But the act setting up the local ombuds-man – as he was quickly and naturally described – provided as in the senior counterpart's case, only for the querying of individual cases of discrimination. Thus if a Catholic – or a Protestant for that matter – felt he had been unfairly treated, he could refer his case to the ombudsman for investigation. But a whole community could not refer their plight to investigation. Thus Fermanagh county, gerry-mandered and palpably stuffed with anti-Catholic dis-crimination, could do nothing. In the county for example, although there is a majority Catholic population – and a working-class one at that – Cameron could cite the fol-lowing : 'In County Fermanagh no senior council posts (and relatively few others) were held by Catholics : this was rationalised by reference to "proven loyalty" as a necessary test for local authority appointments. In that county, among 75 drivers of school buses, at most seven were Catholics. This would appear to be a very clear case of sectarian and political discrimination.' And, incidentally, Fermanagh County Council continues in operation, alive and well, under the chairmanship of Captain John Brooke, a former Stormont Cabinet Minister. If Catholics counted for nothing in Northern politics, they counted for even less in Fermanagh where they had a paper majority.

In Fermanagh there is a sizeable overall Catholic majority on the electoral register. Need more be said? Except that the impression created, and it was unmis-takeable, that the idea of an ombudsman was to end dis-crimination in housing and employment, was quickly and mercilessly cut down when it was found that both offices were practically useless and served little or no reforming purpose.

Allied to the moves to look into local and central dis-crimination there were commitments in the communiqué to the effect that efforts would be made where necessary to eliminate any discrimination in public employment. The ombudsman was given power to look into civil service matters, the Ministry of Community Relations was allowed to seek declarations from those in any way involved in

88

public employment matters, that their policy was one of ensuring equality of employment opportunity without regard to religious or political considerations. The same Ministry was also charged with the responsibility of ensuring that statutory bodies adopted codes of practice and procedure in employment matters. Other minor alterations involving small commissions to oversee employment in the civil service and other parts of the public sector were also introduced.

Against all this the Unionist-dominated state had of course a history studded with the most remarkable sectarian utterances from its Ministers and Prime Ministers, not to mention its MPs, public representatives at other levels and of course its Orangemen. But even without going into the history of fifty years of sectarian statements a simple examination two and a half years after the Downing Street declaration shows what little has changed.

The spirit of the Downing Street declaration had been clearly stated as one designed to provide equality of treatment and opportunity in public and private employment, housing matters, franchise and other areas. But the situation at the present time hardly demonstrates significant change at all: there are very few, if any, Catholics holding any senior rank in any of the establishment divisions of any Ministry, in the private office in any Ministry, in the senior ranks of the professional grades of the Ministry of Finance and the overall picture is that the proportion of Catholics in the administrative and professional grades of the civil service is negligible. Catholics, for example, constitute forty-five per cent of the school population in Northern Ireland. Yet there are only seven Catholics among the fifty-one school inspectors in the Ministry of Education. And this situation obtains still, because even with direct rule the make-up of the civil service and the Stormont Ministries generally, remains almost totally intact with the new British Ministers simply doubling-up for the former Stormont Ministers. And the fact that, by introducing the ombudsman procedure, the authorities may have nipped in the bud further discriminatory practices, is of relatively little use to this or even the next generation. The imbalances and anomalies nourished by the operation of the system will take, even with positive enthusiasm, perhaps fifty years to correct.

The move which provided for local authorities having points schemes for housing allocations and the eventual centralising of housing matters in a central housing executive were, and continue to be, good ideas. A council with a points scheme cannot, unless it is very slippery indeed, avoid allocating houses fairly. Reforms were also promised, and in letter at least implemented, in the fields of community relations. Certainly there was fair speed in setting up the Ministry of Community Relations which was in operation by the end of October following the August 1969 promise. But such a Ministry, given little funds, could do little except by way of social welfare. It talked a lot, not so much under the Unionist, Robert Simpson, but certainly under the Labour man, David Bleakley, who succeeded Simpson when Faulkner came to power in March 1971. Bleakley made regular and thoughtful efforts to at least put the issues before the public. He was the most available of Ministers as even Unionist MPs will testify and when he resigned two days before his term was due to run out in order to draw attention to his opposition to internment he could claim at least to have tried his best. But the whole idea of a Ministry of Community Relations and the emphasis placed on it by the government was sufficient to downgrade this reform to the level of a very minor one indeed. Not that the idea itself was good, bad or indifferent: it was pretty much of a non-idea. When Bleakley took office he said he thought the Ministry should be the litmus for legislation. If government plans were dipped in his Ministry and failed to pass the test they should be abandoned. There is no evidence that any government proposals went through this particular process and indeed some of the Prime Ministerial statements from Faulkner and more than the occasional speech from his Minister of Agriculture, Harry

West, would have failed common decency tests let alone tests of community relations.

Much of the work of the Ministry was involved in fields that would properly be assigned to a Social Services Ministry and the thinking behind this was simply that these areas offered the best hope for involving what was to be – or so the Government pretended – a key Ministry. In fact today it is difficult to point to anything that the Ministry achieved despite goodwill and hard work throughout its offices. If even making the smallest inroads on the tensions between the two communities was even only a part of its purpose then it has failed lamentably. The state of community tensions today is if anything worse than ever and as well as Catholic and Protestant alienation, the alienation of Catholics from the system has been added to the problem. In this respect, ironically, the Ministry became only another government agency from which to be alienated when the time came.

The Community Relations Commission set up at the same time got a vigorous Catholic chairman in Maurice Hayes, town clerk of Downpatrick. But even the commission for the reasons already mentioned in relation to the Ministry, and despite less identification with the system by virtue of its breaking out into several artistic and creative fields, has failed also to be a significant force for reform in Northern society at any level.

In this general field too, there was placed onto the Northern statute book The Prevention of Incitement to Religious Hatred Act. It does not work, it means nothing and it would make no difference whatever if it had never been placed on the statute book in the first instance. The Stormont Attorney-General, Mr Basil Kelly, gave once in parliament an eloquent exposition of why this Act is a piece of legislative nonsense which is no more a reform than would an Act to outlaw Sin by Thought be a reform.

'In order to found a prosecution', he told MPs on 3 February 1971, 'under section one of the Act, one must, firstly, show that the words published or used are threatening, abusive or insulting. But this is only the start. One must then show that they are likely to stir up hatred – not, as I have said, simply distaste or odium – and stir up hatred not against an individual or a number of persons but against a section of the public of Northern Ireland. And, further, this hatred must be hatred against people, not against a religious denomination or a church or a society, secret or otherwise.

'Then, there is perhaps the most important element of all, and in many cases the most difficult of proof, that the person who, when he publishes or uses the words must have the intent to stir up hatred against a section of the public in Northern Ireland. . . .

'In other words – and the Hon. Members opposite must recognise this – a person may use abusive language which is likely to stir up racial or religious hatred but the circumstances may show that he had no intent to stir up racial or religious hatred.'

Thus, out of the mouth of the chief law officer of Northern Ireland, the Act is plainly seen to be a farce. The one prosecution brought under it in the life of its time on the statute book failed completely. And as Mr. Justice Scarman was to point out in his report in April 1972 : 'Those who live in a free country must accept as legitimate the powerful expression of views opposed to their own even if as often happens, it is accompanied by exaggeration, scurrility and abuse.'

On nearly every single point, therefore, but most tragically and vitally, on the important points, what was called 'reform' by successive Unionist governments and indeed by successive Westminster and Dublin governments which didn't bother to make any study of them, was either not reform in the accepted sense of that word as meaning 'change for the better', or was so badly implemented or not implemented at all or was so impractical or unacceptable to either side in the North as to be meaningless, or was so plainly ham-fisted and ill-conceived and poorly-thought out as to have the direct opposite effect to that planned by its proposers. Reform in fact was a failure and failed to make any significant impression on the problems of Northern Ireland. It tinkered with ideas on paper, put them in some cases into print and then found that either they didn't work or, if they did, their workings meant little or nothing to anybody. Reform did not bring one new job to the North, it did not heighten the standard of living – true it did not lower it either, but that would have been so even without reform – but most vitally it did absolutely nothing to give the working-class Catholic any reason to feel identified with the system which governed him. And if he didn't identify why should he bother to restrain himself, to be amenable to the law, to co-operate with the system in any way?

The false hope that there was a new deal had been held out in the Autumn of 1969 by two governments, but especially by the British Labour government which had sent soldiers to the Catholics' rescue and had stripped the Unionist masters of their B men and taken guns from the police. But it was only a short time before the discovery that he was still a second-class citizen was confirmed in the mind of the ghetto-Catholic. And the ghettoes would set the pace.

Open hostility to a system is a good breeding ground for those who will organise for that system's overthrow. When that hostility is fed by disillusionment then the organisation of opposition is made that bit easier. So the civil disobedience campaign that began after internment had a fertile field in which the seeds were well under root and only the harvest needed to be gathered. In coming together in such massive numbers to oppose internment, the Catholic community was at one and the same time finding a vehicle for opposition to the measure itself and a method of demonstrating its total disillusionment with the whole system. In the early days of the campaign after internment the remarks one most often heard after condemnation of internment were in clear terms suggestions that nothing had changed since 1968. The British troops on the streets rounding up the opponents of Stormont seemed to be the final proof of this sentiment.

Nothing is ever simple in Northern Ireland. It is generally an understatement of some size to suggest that there is only one or two meanings to everything done and said. But the failure of reform must rank as a major factor in the eventual downfall of the system. When something, internment in this case, arrived to channel the bitterness and disappointment with this failure, its significance would be seen to the full. Thus at one and the same time internment was an evil in itself, a factor in the downfall. And, while there were others, the chief reason it was so was because of its unifying force on the disillusioned Catholic population. As the wicked month of August limped out on a bomb and a bullet the system was hard on its heels.

6 FAULKNER'S SECOND EFFORT

The policy of internment had definitely come to stay. By early September as every sign was being read and re-read by political commentators and politicians themselves for a hint of any move on the policy the strongest suggestion that it would be of a semi-permanent nature could be gleaned from the building at Long Kesh and the daily, sometimes even hourly, rounding-up of suspects. As internment dug in its heels so did the civil disobedience campaign, the Opposition and the Catholic community generally. Violence went on unabated. After a month of internment not only was there no let-up in the campaign of death and explosion but a new impetus had been given to it by the internment policy. Tortuous efforts were made by politicians at Stormont and in Westminster to explain away, by juggling facts and figures, the continuing escalation of the security crisis. For a time the rate of bombings dropped slightly and there were a few less killings but overall there was never at any time between August and Christmas a lull in the violence. Every imaginable type of incident occurred: more policemen were shot, UDR men were killed, soldiers were killed, civilians died in shooting incidents and bomb blasts, booby-traps killed army explosive experts, there were literally days on which a dozen armed robberies would net their perpetrators up to £10,000 in Belfast or Derry, post office vans were held up and robbed, installations as well as commercial premises were blown up, there were daylight bombings, afternoon bombings, bomb hoaxes that sent towns and cities into chaos and gradually but perceptibly the entire life of Northern Ireland was being drawn more and more into the action. Shops closed early, so did pubs. Hotels reported a massive fall-off in trade.

In the streets of the towns and cities the notices 'Bomb Sale' or 'Business as Usual' were pinned to hardboard shutters which took the place of smashed windows. Troops patrolled the streets continually, there were delays of hours at times as cars were stopped and rigorously searched and perpetual appeals went to the public in all walks of life for co-operation with the security forces. Once at a press conference in October the Prime Minister Mr Faulkner swung angrily on a reporter who suggested Northern Ireland was 'being governed by the bomb and the bullet'. The Prime Minister hotly denied this and pointed to continuing industrial life as the type of normal activity that was keeping the North going. It was a brave effort to put a face on a bad situation. In fact by September-October Northern Ireland was a desperate place indeed: apart from the type of scene outlined above there was no hope at any level. Politicians were more rather than less estranged, the communities – at levels where it mattered in the ghettoes – were still divided in their dealings by the peace-lines and in their minds and hearts by the accumulated bitterness of two years combined with the ever-available reservoir of antagonisms handed down from generation to generation. By the time the House of Commons at Stormont was resuming after the summer recess the tiny state was split in two on every single issue of importance. One got the impression at times that it would split even if it were suggested that black was white. Not even on that could it agree.

As Faulkner and his ministers took their places after the recess the face of parliamentary democracy was saved by the newly-formed Democratic Unionist party led by Ian Paisley and Desmond Boal. They crossed the floor of the Commons and, occupying the seats of SDLP and Nationalist MPs, became the Opposition. And some Opposition too! On their first outing Boal particularly tore strips off the Unionist party and government on the single issue of the government's move against councils where absenteeism had prevented the holding of meetings and where the government now proposed to replace existing local authorities with commissions or boards under the auspices of the Ministry of Development. Stormont showed itself in poor light that day as the Minister of Development, Roy Bradford, ran back and forth to the civil servants' box to try and find out whether they even understood some of the points Boal was making. And when he would return triumphant with an answer Boal would produce another question. It was as near to a farce as the Commons had ever seen.

As Stormont reassembled of course it did so under more than a few shadows. September had seen the twelve-point plan for a 'New Ireland' proposed by Mr Harold Wilson in a speech in London. Much of the speech was hardly feasible in the Northern situation and particularly the emphasis Wilson gave to eventual reunification in his speech did nothing to woo Unionist hearts and minds. Mr Wilson would later repeat the main points in November but the fact was that a leader of the Opposition in Britain had now put unity and many other anti-Unionist ideas into the light of public discussion. And in September too Faulkner had suffered the embarrassing resignation of Bleakley from his cabinet two days before the term of office allowed to him as a non-MP was due to run out. Bleakley said in his resignation letter that he had decided to resign because of internment. He wrote :

'I believe that internment is wrong, that this aspect of our policy is a tragic mistake which has made matters worse; further I believe that the terrorists welcome internment for it gives the IRA and other militant groups a sympathy and hearing on a world-wide scale which otherwise they could not get. In addition the internment controversy handicaps those who are presenting the Northern Ireland case against the campaign of violence. There are of course many arguments which one could produce on the subject but at this stage I stress the one that involved me most as Minister of Community Relations – the effect on Protestant-Catholic relationships.

97

'Internment is not, as many see it, an isolated security issue: it is a test of policy direction. More than any other single issue it separates Protestant and Roman Catholic and tragically has alienated the Roman Catholic community at the very moment when community co-operation is most vital. In fact in Ulster today we just cannot have internment *and* a united community. And without a united community a really worthwhile province is impossible.'

Bleakley's resignation was a blow to Faulkner. He had hoped that the Labour man would stay the full term and leave it at that but the realisation of what internment had done was spelled out by Bleakley as he left for simple reasons. As Minister for Community Relations he had spent the last month of his six-month period touring bombed areas of the city, particularly Catholic areas where incessantly the message he got was of opposition to internment. And even in Protestant areas as the violence continued he got a puzzled message from those who wondered: is it working? are the IRA being beaten and caught? is it just as bad as ever? So from both sides the message of internment's failure came in: it had split Catholics from authority, split the two communities and received only milk-and-water support from the Protestants. The divisions it created between the two communities were brought home to Bleakley as he realised on his tours that Protestants gave it what support they did out of their reserve of natural inclination to support a Unionist government. This, again, inevitably put them on the other side of the fence from Catholics. Reconciliation was further away than ever.

In the last few days of September the much-talked of tripartite talks between Faulkner, Heath and Jack Lynch took place at Chequers. It is hard even looking back now to see what useful purpose they served. Each man came away telling his supporters he had stood for their rights, particularly Lynch and Faulkner. But it was clear that very little had been achieved. As parliament settled down to business at Stormont it was announced that the Opposition groups who had left that assembly were pressing ahead vigorously with their plans for an alternative assembly which they had announced when they withdrew in July. Mr John Hume, the MP for Foyle, was to be President of the new assembly which would, it was announced, meet in Derry on 5 October, the third anniversary of the first famous civil rights march. In the event those plans had to be changed and the Assembly, with the amazingly pretentious title 'The Assembly of the Northern Irish People,' had to wait until later in the month for its first meeting. But getting it off the ground at all was yet another public blow to Faulkner and to Stormont. Even if it did turn out to be a 'Catholic Parliament for a Catholic people', it exemplified the divisions in the community at elected level. It didn't help the Faulkner fight to save Stormont. And that fight was now very much underway. All the strands that had been gathered together by internment – the polarisation of the Catholic community, the intransigence of the elected leaders of Catholic opinion and the growing evidence of the policy's basic failures – were beginning to act strongly on the Stormont system as each day passed. And violence continued. What had begun in 1969 as Catholic reaction to Protestant attack and had grown through opposition to the British army was now in a new phase, post-internment. The first reaction against the policy itself was in a way over. But the IRA, especially the Provisionals, were far from finished. In fact their quite incredible successes had encouraged them. Violence was yet to play its most important role by continuing.

The part played by violence and force of arms in the eventual downfall of the whole Stormont system is, self-evidently, of major importance. Basically, little if anything would have been done by politicians if there had not been a campaign of violence by, principally, the Provisional IRA. When, after direct rule had been announced, Faulkner said that many people in Britain might draw a sinister message from the British government decision to the effect that violence could and in fact did pay, he was being more honest and coming a lot closer to the truth than those politicians, mainly from the non-Unionist side, who came before television cameras to claim credit for the moves or to suggest that they had come about through political manoeuvrings. There cannot be any doubt about the part played by violence. After August 1969 there were only the feeble beginnings of the organisation which was to develop into the Provisional IRA. On the ground it would flourish, but slowly, as the politicians failed to come up with change and progress. And the stupidities and ineptitude of the British Army led to a situation where those people who preached tolerance, understanding of the Army's role and the view that things had changed and were changing, were gradually isolated in the Catholic community as incident after incident reduced the acceptability of the Army. For example: it was still genuinely possible before July 1970 to find whole areas of the Catholic population even in the ghettoes at least feeling in some way sympathetic to the Army, the British government and the difficulties both were facing. The Falls curfew, the result of panic and over-reaction by the GOC Freeland changed this situation over a weekend.

Thus it was to some extent initial violence from the British Army which alienated the population. As events developed and the Provisionals would commit some new 'atrocity' it only needed the subsequent over-reaction by the Army to swing back to the gunman the sympathy he might have lost in the first instance. Violence and counter-violence, reaction and counter-reaction and over-reaction were bound up in each other. This was the pattern of violence in the early seventies. What began as protection duty from the Provisionals could then of course quite easily swing into full-scale military campaigning for political ends. Throughout the final months of 1970 the cautious optimism from the security forces was to the effect that things were getting better. But in autumn of that year anti-Army rioting, usually for localised reasons, drew the Army into conflict first with the local population and then with the growing IRA. By the spring of

1971 the huge-scale riots of the 'old days' with bottle, stone and petrol bomb were giving way to a campaign of bombing and shooting. This in turn brought more military activity and more military activity encouraged people to seek other ways than force to end the impasse. But there would have been no impasse if it hadn't been for the violence. Suppose for example that the Opposition had left parliament, the community had gone on civil disobedience and the Catholic people had decided not to co-operate with authority but things had remained peaceful? If life wasn't affected too badly the attitude of government could have been: so what? Why bother if things are only being disorganised? But when lives are being lost it is a different matter. And with the North virtually on the brink of war it was inevitable that more lives would be lost.

It has been as hard for Catholics in Northern Ireland to accept the security forces and their behaviour over the last three years as it is for other sections of the community to come to terms with the phenomenon of the IRA Provisionals. But both are violent, both are armies and armies are for killing and being killed. When a civilian population stands between two armies, afraid of both, it is natural that one section will identify with one army and the other with the second army, in varying degrees of support. Again, the middle-class Catholic, either in elected office or in private, indulges in almost ritual condemnation of the violence of both Army and IRA but at the same time will not hand the IRA over to authority. His mouthings about violence and his supposed abhorrence of it matter little while violence continues in the community. Men who use violence are not mad, not deranged, they are not the 'animals' they are called. They use it for politics, in much the same way as politicians use parliamentary methods: as a tactic. There has been much heated discussion about violence in Northern Ireland, particularly from the Unionist side. The Provisional IRA are not animals, not mad men, no more than the obvious and expected products of violence through the years in Northern Ireland. If the gun and the threat to use it could bring the state into existence then the gun and the same threat could knock it out of existence again. It is as tragically simple and easy to understand as that. And, for bonus, the myths, the legends and the twisting of history by selective fact-finding can be admitted in evidence by both sides.

Apart from on the ground support for the IRA and violence from Catholic ghetto areas the mentality among the middle-class was such as never to betray the IRA intellectually. Basically most Catholics in Northern Ireland want a united Ireland in some shape or form some day. The IRA wants the same only quicker. For many Catholics then the dilemma is that they disagree with the IRA only on tactics and since these tactics are the same type as those employed by the British Army the idea of attacking them outright or in public becomes less compulsive. There is a strange phenomenon in Northern Irish Catholic politics: whereas the elected MPs privately explain their very necessary vested interest in violence but publicly condemn it, the ordinary individual is squeamish about violence in private but will never openly attack its perpetrators. During the last two years, and especially the last year, when Stormont was teetering on the brink of collapse, this was manifestly obvious. The SDLP for example has 'always condemned' violence in politics. But it has rarely meant what it says to the letter. When Gerry Fitt rules out the prospect of the IRA being included in peace negotiations all he is really saying is that the IRA has done its part of the job and the politicians who are, according to themselves, cleverer men, should be allowed to get on with the rest of it. Implicitly he recognises the part played by violence to bring him and his political colleagues so far along the road. It is clear that for the last year in Northern Ireland's parliamentary life the politicians on the Catholic side ritually condemned violence while knowing that they had a genuine need for its continuance if their political views were to carry weight. In essence violence and more polite forms of activity are complementary in politics.

And if this general rule holds true it is even more accurate in Northern Ireland. The whole progress of the British government, for example towards the eventual direct rule decision, was dictated as much by violence as by any pressure on them from politicians in the North, in Dublin or at Westminster to act as they did. Thus after internment and the violence it produced the British government began to talk openly and more freely about the need for political initiative. The old Maudling line about 'an active permanent and guaranteed role for the Catholic people in the life and current affairs of Northern Ireland' was to give way to rumours about community government, a secretary of state for Northern Ireland and other such ideas. After the holocaust in Derry on Sunday 30 January when thirteen civilians were killed by British troops the Westminster government was moved further along the direct rule road and it was becoming clear that the 'last resort' policy was more and more in politicians' minds. Both Labour and Conservative governments had always said that the imposition of direct rule would only be done as a last resort but events developed so quickly in the first eleven weeks of this year that the last resort was being reached at speed when Britain eventually decided to move. Incidents like the February assassination attempt on the life of John Taylor, the Junior Home Affairs Minister at Stormont, served only to heighten the need for action as the IRA showed no sign at all of cooling the situation. Indeed things had gone straight into open war after internment by which time every member of the security forces was a fair target for the IRA and daily bombings were done as much to keep the security forces tense as to try and upset the nerves of the community.

As violence continued unabated, however, politics did not take a silent backseat. In late October the Prime Minister introduced his long-awaited Green Paper on the future of parliamentary government in Northern Ireland.

Faulkner's proposals were very weak on this occasion. There was a repetition of the idea of committee systems for the House of Commons, a suggestion that the commons and senate themselves might be enlarged and some slight hint that there could be a re-introduction of the system of proportional representation for elections to both parliament and local authorities. But there was a clear indication that the Faulkner government considered that the idea of a form of community government could only be in the context of invitations from a Unionist Prime Minister to outsiders to join his government and not on a basis of non-Unionists joining a government as of right. On the same day as the Green Paper came out the Opposition 'Assembly of the Northern Irish People' met for the first time in Dungiven in Co. Derry. It promised to try to provide a forum for non-Unionist opinion in the North but with the Stormont parliament now visibly reduced to a Protestant parliament for a Protestant people, the Dungiven assembly was no more than a Catholic version for the Catholic community. Only Ivan Cooper and Senator Claude Wilton, two Protestants, upset the sectarian make-up of the Opposition assembly. It was a ludicrous spectacle on both sides: Stormont and Dungiven shouting insults across the Bann at each other while violence and fear rampaged the countryside.

The day after the Green Paper and the Dungiven meeting Faulkner dropped a bombshell by announcing that Dr G. B. Newe, a former social worker and a Catholic, was joining his cabinet as a Minister of State in his own department. Newe agreed at a press conference a day later that he didn't represent anybody, that he wouldn't try and claim to do so and that he was in effect joining the cabinet to try and co-operate with the government in bringing about reconciliation in the community. He said he hoped to try and take the 'rough edges' out of the internment policy but could not elaborate. Newe was bitterly attacked: Michael Farrell the PD leader likened his job to that of a Jew in Hitler's cabinet, the SDLP scoffed and sneered at him and Unionists were

104

either unmoved by the appointment or else welcomed it, fully realising that it meant nothing at all in the context at the time. No-one was impressed with Newe's appointment but at least it meant that Faulkner had given the Unionists a look at the thin end of one wedge: a Catholic in the Orangeman's power-centre after fifty years was an innovation, but only by putting a very favourable complexion such as that on the move can Faulkner's idea be seen as anything other than a crude political gimmick designed to try to woo the middle-class Catholics away from opposition to internment, to government and – as was rapidly happening – to the whole system. As for Newe personally, it was certainly a courageous decision to accept the post: a generally popular figure he presumably felt that if introducing a word or two of Catholic thinking into the Protestant cabinet helped the general situation then he could do it as well as the next man.

But the appointment did nothing to ease the situation. Not a bomb or bullet stayed put because of it and if, coupled with the Green Paper, it was meant as a sort of double-edged effort to change the situation it failed completely. The Provisional IRA campaign continued, the 'atrocities' went on daily, there were continual arrest operations, shootings between troops and civilians in Catholic areas and of course border incidents involving hit and run attacks from the Republic into the North.

Strange though it may seem the actual physical border as such had not figured prominently in the IRA campaign until in September the British Army, acting purely politically, had agreed to the surprising policy of blowing up cross border roads and culverts to try and stop the IRA in frontier areas from crossing into the North. The operation was ludicrous on several counts and was devalued by the source from which it had sprung: Taylor. An inveterate hardline Unionist, Taylor, who earlier had made the speech threatening resignation if the IRA were not beaten fairly quickly, had floated the idea of road-cratering in a speech in late August and although the idea had been scoffed at by military experts as being bad on several grounds he pressed it so hard within the cabinet that he got his way eventually. The blowing up of cross-border roads was to provoke many incidents along the border with the Republic, provoke reaction from the Dublin government which objected strongly to the measure, and, ultimately, to prove of no great use to the North's security forces in their battle with the two wings of the IRA. Cratering had the effect, too, of bringing into focus the relationship between the two parts of the country and of demonstrating how much those relations had deteriorated since the heady and exciting days when Seán Lemass, then Taoiseach, had crossed the border to meet the Stormont Prime Minister, O'Neill. Later, when Lynch became Taoiseach, he too travelled to Stormont.

Events in August 1969 had produced massive emotional reaction in the Republic and Lynch had moved his troops close to the border during the fierce rioting in Derry. Irish Army field hospitals had been set up; Dublin, Cork and other centres received their quota of refugees and after Lynch had made a statement saying his government and people could not 'stand idly by', Chichester-Clark, already shaken by the incidents in Derry and Belfast, appeared at a news conference to tell Ireland, Britain and the world: 'We must now look elsewhere for our friends.' It was the last hope gone. Not since then have the leaders of the Dublin or Stormont governments exchanged any form of friendly greetings. Even if behind the scenes at Stormont and the Dáil both leaders might privately have recognised each other's problems with hardliners in the ruling parties, the climate of friendly co-operation could never return.

Apart from the decision not to intern it would be difficult to see 'the hand of Dublin' in the downfall of Stormont, but the fact that Mr Lynch and his colleagues turned a blind eye to any upsurge for IRA support in the Republic, made no attempt to ease Stormont's burden on the political front, and generally adopted a policy of 'no policy', allied to regular diplomatic pressures on London and at the United Nations, may have played a minor role. Certainly Dublin was good at turning out publicity, for the most part, be it said, accurate, which reflected poorly on the Stormont administration. World-wide dissemination of news of the situation in the North was spread by Irish embassies and agencies abroad and at home every effort at co-operation was made with the Northern Opposition who had frequent meetings with Lynch.

But while Dublin reacted to events in the North it never acted positively, it never showed in black and white what exactly it had, or has now, in mind for the future united Ireland of which it dreams. A charitable reading of this is that the Dublin politicians have no desire to show their hand, believe the problem is for the British and will make their move at the appropriate time. But a more realistic interpretation is that, having never believed at any time up to 1968 that things would change north of the border, the Fianna Fáil government was so much caught on the hop by the spiral of events that it never regained its feet sufficiently to think out a coherent policy for the whole country. Certainly the whirlwind of events over the past three to four years has left Dublin standing as far as constructive ideas are concerned. When it did produce ideas they rarely seemed to have sympathy for the human beings who professed Unionism in the North. One can understand one set of politicians not feeling any moral duty to rescue another set in distress but in the last few years there has been a very evident lack of feeling in Dublin over the years for the North and the Northerner. The Dublin Government's contacts, for example, seemed to be and still appear to be exclusively Catholic/Nationalist: thus John Hume and Austin Currie will meet Mr Lynch's aides and advisers when the latter travel North or the Northern MPs go to Dublin. But there has never been a strong contact established between Mr Lynch's government and the Unionist party, never a genuine link with the Protestant population at grass-roots level or in the ghettoes. If men like Hume, Currie and Devlin were to be consulted, why not men like Boal, McQuade, Paisley and even official Unionists in or out of government? Some of them live only miles across the border from Fianna Fáil TDs and Ministers in border counties but they have never even met to discuss the Irish problem.

To sum up the Dublin attitude over the past few years it would appear that while only a hundred miles separates Dublin from Belfast, the distance has to all intents and purposes been light years. It is years, for example, since a Dáil committee was set up to examine and report on the 1937 Constitution of the Republic, regarded rightly or wrongly by Northern Protestants as a sectarian document. The Republic too has its discriminatory sectarian laws. In December this point was emphasised by Paisley in the course of long interviews with RTE and in the *Irish Times* and *Irish Press*. He pointed to the Republic's 1937 Constitution and said that if those parts of it which were by their very nature, sectarian, indeed, if the whole Constitution which he dubbed 'theocratic in a Roman Catholic context,' were changed there could be 'good neighbourliness in the strictest sense of the word' between North and South. As soon as he had said it Paisley was accused of flirting with Republicans and his statement was twisted by Unionists. In fact what he had said was nothing that many Protestants hadn't been saying for a long time : the important point was that Paisley said it. But his words fell on deaf ears. Not a word from Mr Lynch or any Dublin minister. Not a kite flown from even a Fianna Fáil backbencher. The arch-ogre of the early days could say what he wanted, Dublin didn't seem to care. It was another missed opportunity. One Fine Gael Senator, Mr John Maurice Kelly, who took it upon himself to reply to Paisley, said in so many words that he did not believe the Bann Side MP, and went on to say that the day he saw Protestants in the North vote for a united Ireland he would begin to think about changing the Constitution of the Republic. More people than Kelly have failed to realise that there will never be Protestant co-operation as long as the 1937 Constitution remains in operation.

There are other points too where the relations between the two states in Ireland have been brought into focus in the last few years and where, to say the least, the South has been conspicuously lacking in effort and enthusiasm. If the price of a united Ireland were to depend on change in the Republic one wonders whether Southern leaders would buy.

Attitudes in the Republic, however, were not of major significance in the downfall of Stormont except in the areas mentioned earlier : refusal to intern and support and encouragement for the Opposition. The Dublin government had internment as a policy in its political locker and indeed still has : its demands for an end to the Special Powers Act, for example, are generally followed in Dublin by Sinn Féin demands for an end to the Offences Against the State Act which carries, among other penal clauses, the right to intern without trial. It does seem now, however, that had the Dublin government of the past three years been genuinely far-seeing, eager and enthusiastic with regard to the Northern crisis the changes it could have brought about would have been at once acceptable to Northern Catholics, assuaged the fears of the Protestants and, in that way, made the day of eventual reconciliation perhaps come nearer. Government by promise from Dublin has at times been just as bad as government by promise North of the border. Reform in the Republic is something which could well bear immediate examination and perhaps the application there of as many inquiries as the North has had in its time would produce some equally dramatic changes.

Even now in the post-direct rule period there has been little movement from Dublin. Mr Lynch was surely wise to bide his time in reacting but private suggestions from Dublin that the time is now accepted as ripe for 'extending the hand of friendship' have not been followed by any discernible actions from the government. Admittedly Dublin's task of getting across to the mainstreams of Unionism is a formidable, if not perhaps an altogether impossible one.

Faulkner, for example, is now leader of the Unionist party and not a Prime Minister, but this should hardly be allowed to stand in the way of some contact being made between politicians on both sides of the border who would not normally be on the same side of the political fence.

But long before the time that Paisley had made his remarks about the Republic, in December, the point of stalemate had been reached in Northern politics. Moves seemed impossible for the politicians and the pace was continually being set, as it had been for months, by violence.

7 ENTER 1972:
VANGUARD AND BLOODY SUNDAY

By the time he had offered his Green Paper and put Newe in the cabinet Faulkner had nothing more to offer, no new ideas. No-one took very much notice of Newe and the Green Paper was either ignored, as by the Catholics, or criticised for not meaning much, as by Desmond Boal. In a House of Commons speech Boal said it was obvious that the aims of the Green Paper were to attract Catholics and offer them some involvement in running affairs. But he poured scorn on the proposals, saying that if he were a Catholic he wouldn't be particularly impressed with what was being offered. Faulkner was all the time searching for a new initiative himself, for a new impetus he might give to the situation which would win back respect and support for parliament. But everything that happened went against him and his aims.

In November, the committee set up under Sir Edmund Compton to investigate allegations of brutality against the security forces on men arrested in the first 48 hours of the August internment operation reported. It found all the allegations true, but chose to call them 'ill-treatment' rather than 'brutality'. It found that men had been forced to stay awake, had been deprived of food and proper drink after their arrest, had been forced to stand in awkward positions, had been kept isolated and generally had been subject to severe physical and mental pressures. Faulkner, at the time in August that the first claims had been made, had denied any such activity on behalf of the security forces. Now yet another committee had found fault with the Stormont administration. This time it involved the security forces acting under the Special Powers Act.

As usual the problems were security ones but the old crux was now even more in evidence : the troops were

111

British but their tasks were being done for the Northern Irish government, clearly an administration which did not have the confidence of either the Protestant or Catholic communities. And Britain's hands were becoming increasingly soiled as pressure all over the world mounted for some form of 'initiative' aimed at healing divisions and restoring the community to peace. In the run-up to Christmas the air was full of speculation. Searching for an initiative became the new political game played by everyone and the stories from London began to leak as through a colander.

In late October the London Editor of the *Irish Times*, James Downey, ran an exclusive story saying that direct rule of Northern Ireland was being contemplated by the British government. I well remember meeting Ian Paisley in the corridors at Stormont the day after the story. He laughed and said the report was way off the mark: his ear was close to the Westminster ground and no such move was being contemplated. But, whether connected or not, Paisley himself dropped a massive bombshell two weeks later when he announced that he had firm and reliable information that direct rule was to be imposed, that there would be a secretary of state for Northern Ireland and that the person to fill the job would be Christopher Soames, British Ambassador in Paris. The story was never denied. The phrases 'pure speculation' and 'groundless opinion' were used but Paisley repeated his statement again and again. In an evening sermon in his Belfast church he spelled out the attitude he advocated to the move he forecast.

He told his congregation that direct rule was on the way in 'weeks rather than months', that it would be a sad day for Ulstermen but that there was nothing they could do about it. The next day he said: 'There is no comparison now with the 1912 situation. We have no Edward Carson, there is no division at Westminster between the two parties and there is no army to mutiny.' He added on this last point, rather ruefully: 'There won't even be a private to desert over this.' As matters were to turn out later Paisley

112

was almost completely accurate and his London informant must have been extremely reliable. There is equally no doubt that Downey's story was correct too : direct rule was firmly in the British Cabinet's mind. The Protestant backlash had been among the fears underlined but when Paisley came out with his statement in such resigned and acquiescent terms a sigh of relief passed from those ministers in favour of the direct rule proposal. For if there was to be a Protestant backlash of serious proportions then Paisley would be in the forefront. If he was prepared to take it, if not lying down then at least with resignation the Protestant reaction would consequently be less difficult to handle. The logic of fighting the British to keep the British connection was something which Paisley knew would be difficult to get across to Protestants even if he had believed it himself. From that moment direct rule drew even nearer. Faulkner was deeper in trouble and Stormont was toppling even more shakily.

There now followed a period of intense speculation about the 'initiative'. Every politician and every British and Irish newspaper tried their hand at forecasting. From London there came regular stories, leaks, hints and suggestions some of which bordered on the ludicrous and can only have been leaked for the prime purpose of testing Protestant reaction in the crudest possible manner. Thus there were stories about community government based loosely on the Maudling statement of months back about an 'active, permanent and guaranteed role for Catholics in the life and public affairs of Northern Ireland'. A *Sunday Times* story would one day forecast that the British government had decided to have Stormont so restructured that there would have to be a Catholic vice-premier and that some cabinet posts would be retained especially for Catholics; the next day some other newspaper foresaw proportional representation, a council of Ireland, a secretary of state or at least a special minister to look after the Northern Ireland counter at the Home Office and so on. Some papers even reported a plan for repartition. As each new story appeared Faulkner would take refuge in the

Green Paper, the original idea of the committee system extension in the Commons and the need to defeat the IRA militarily. As usual Stormont ministers, especially Faulkner, spoke about the imminent defeat of the IRA. Faulkner had of course never stopped talking about this and newspaper headlines through his career are peppered with such phrases as : 'PM sees defeat near for terrorists' and the like. In Britain too there was generally the same type of baseless optimism.

No matter what the IRA did some Unionist would see in it cause for hope that the campaign was nearing an end. If the Provisionals perpetrated some ghastly deed it was evidence 'that they are desperate men' – never that they were confident they could get away with anything. If they did nothing for a while it was evidence that they were losing support – never that they were simply waiting to seize their next opportunity. The most typical situation of this type occurred in early December when about 150 Provisionals took part one Saturday in a spate of almost thirty bombings in two hours, causing havoc along the border, in Belfast, Derry and other towns and killing three people and injuring scores. The official government line? That the IRA had been losing support but had been forced to put on a show of strength to bolster flagging morale. The more perceptive and honest admitted that it was a sinister and ominous piece of evidence to support the theory that the North was being run by the Provisionals in every way and they could turn their campaign on and off like a tap.

Daily now the situation was deteriorating while men in positions of authority were trying to put across the line that it was getting better. No-go areas in Derry such as the Bogside and Creggan, which not even the British Army would enter, were not just helping the IRA, they were furthering the alienation of the Catholic population by ensuring that they became used to a situation where no state representative of 'law and order' was present. These no-go areas continued right through Mr Faulkner's term of office.

There were appeals to the IRA for a Christmas truce

and for three or four days over the holiday period there was a cessation of violence. Hope was expressed that this could be continued but it was as much to give the IRA and the civilian Catholic population a rest as it was to provide peace. As it was it proved again that the Provos could do pretty well as they pleased. In the last few days of the year Senator John Barnhill, a rather elderly Unionist, was murdered by the Official IRA who called at his house and blew it up. He was shot when he resisted and his body was left in the house which was demolished. The crime infuriated people and it was particularly repellent coming from the Official wing of the IRA which had piously attacked the Provisional campaign as sectarian. It was the type of incident which hammered home that it was simply a waste of time even talking about the effect of such and such an act on community relations. By the time Jack Barnhill was killed nothing that could happen would make the slightest difference to either community. Events would now make no impact, except in Britain on the Westminster government. In Northern Ireland there was stalemate. The government had nothing to offer, the Opposition even less and eyes turned inevitably to the British for a solution.

As 1972 opened Northern Ireland presented a sorry picture to the world. Apart from its blitzed cities and its death toll it had arrived at a point from which forward progress was impossible. It is worth just considering for a moment the way things stood on all fronts as January came to the North.

On the government side the Unionist administration was bankrupt and discredited and had no visible support anywhere. It had gone from being distrusted and disliked by Catholics to being openly hated and detested by almost that entire community. Meanwhile among the Protestant population the failure of internment was being taken as a sign of overall failure: unemployment went up rather than down, industry was driven away, there were no new jobs, no more money and no hope of either on the horizon. The government had lamentably failed to solve the security crisis and worse still, in trying extraordinary measures, it had alienated one entire community and falsely raised the hopes of its supporters. By early 1972 those hopes were in pieces on the ground, admittedly blasted as much by IRA bombs as by government failure. Mr Faulkner's own personality, his style, his viciousness against the IRA and his deviousness had ruined whatever chances he might have had among the two communities and his government was tarred with his brush. There were no moderate voices in the cabinet, no hint that any minister had a single constructive idea to help the situation. Where another government might have asked for help, the Unionists arrogantly continued as before, drawing ministerial salaries, doing little or no work in any field that couldn't have been done – and wasn't anyway – by good civil servants. In other words, by 1972, if it had not been so before, the Unionist government was in the oldest and strictest sense of the word corrupt. It had no mandate from the people, no genuine support and no ultimate hope of survival.

In the Protestant community there was utter despair with the continuing security crisis, the daily and nightly bombings and the apparent and visible failure of the security forces to deal with it. There was growing disappointment with internment, continuing uncertainty about the government, in particular about the Prime Minister who had never had 100 per cent backing from ultra-loyalists, and the first signs that the community in the cities and in the country was feeling cut-off, neglected and friendless. There did not appear to be any real Protestant leader: Paisley had very definitely confused his followers by opposing internment and they wondered too about his new ideas on the Republic's constitution: to hardline Protestants that had been an area outside the pale of discussion and even mentioning it had done Paisley some harm. Faulkner, like his predecessors before him, would be blamed for everything in any event, so he could not lead; Craig alone seemed to have a consistent Unionist and Protestant line, but he had as yet no publicised power base from which to operate. That was coming.

The Catholic community owed the government a round

million pounds in rent and rates; the civil disobedience campaign was stronger than ever and if every Catholic home wasn't quite a no-go area the huge housing estates in Belfast and Derry and every Catholic town in the North were hostile fortresses of resentment, bitterness and hatred. All of which combined to produce total alienation. There wasn't a shred of hope among the population there. As for the Catholic politicians, they were helpless even if they had wanted to assist in any way. Having crystallised the political opposition to internment and in part organised the civil disobedience campaign they were with their people and could not depart from them. As Gerry Fitt said when asked on a BBC programme on the crisis: 'If we talked now we would be representing nobody.' Fitt did not mention that in his original script he had said there could be circumstances in which he would talk even while internment lasted but when his party heard that they ordered him to scrub the reference and when he appeared it was to take the hard line of total opposition to talks until internment was ended and every internee released. Apart from that the Opposition politicians did nothing: they continued their social welfare work for constituents and issued statements about IRA violence, British Army violence, the threat of Protestant violence and so on. They travelled occasionally to Dublin and talked to other politicians. But, regrettably too, they produced no formula that could attract both Protestant and Catholic or ease the situation in any way. Their stand and firmness on internment was commendable but it tended to overshadow all their political thinking and exclude everything else from consideration. Even if it was the single most vital issue it should not have prevented the party, relieved of Stormont duties, from working on future policy plans. They produced none.

The scene which Faulkner surveyed then at the start of the year was one of political desolation and massive community unrest. Cities and towns resembled battle fronts and it is not an exaggeration to say that every square inch of the North was involved in some way or another in day-to-day events. Quiet seaside resorts like Rostrevor in Co. Down were being patrolled by British troops, every RUC station in the country had its barbed wire and sandbags and on the road outside it large humps of tarred gravel were placed to slow down traffic and thus reduce the chances of bombers and gunmen driving past quickly. January, needless to say, was a violent month but nothing that happened in its thirty-one days had anything like the impact of events in Derry city on the afternoon of Sunday 30 January.

The governmental ban on parades and marches had been extended in August 1971 for one year when internment began. But the civil rights associations and anti-internment groups generally decided to hold a massive march in Derry on the last Sunday in January. Against local advice from the RUC chief in the city, Mr Frank Lagan, the Army decided that the illegal march should be contained within the Bogside area and not allowed to enter Guildhall Square. Barricades were accordingly placed by troops across the exit routes from the Bogside and Creggan. The plan, unlike other methods that had been used for other illegal marches, was not to 'note names with a view to prosecution' but to mount an actual arrest operation.

What happened on the day that has passed into history as 'Bloody Sunday' is perhaps better known than any other single event in the last three years in the North. While countless incidents are forgotten the memory that British paratroopers fired into crowds and killed thirteen civilians will linger on. There was never anything like that day in Ireland, certainly not for fifty years anyway. Eventually the mass-killings became the subject of an inquiry set up by the British government under the Lord Chief Justice of England Lord Widgery. He found, most vitally, that despite Army claims that they shot only gunmen or bombers, none of the thirteen was proved to have been handling a firearm or bomb when shot. He went on : 'Some are wholly acquitted of complicity; but there is a strong suspicion that some others had been firing weapons or handling bombs in the course of the afternoon and that yet others had been closely supporting them.' Angry Catholic reaction was to dismiss Widgery as a white-washer. But in his findings, he clearly supported the contention that all killed were innocent. All he could do was cast 'suspicion' on some of them, while completely exonerating most. The Army had quite simply killed innocent people and no semantic juggling or effort to explain away what had happened would alter the fact. As Eddie McAteer, leader of the Nationalist party in Derry, said: 'The Derry people know what happened that day. I suppose we should count ourselves lucky the judge didn't find that all thirteen committed suicide.'

Seemingly endless miles of copy have already been written about the whys and wherefores of that day but the precise details are not important in the context of the impact of events on Stormont. The implications were vast. The Army had not run amok as some claimed. The operation had all the signs of planning and it had been executed by the paratroopers whose record of coolness and unflappability was well-known. The Paras didn't lose their heads that day, they knew what they were doing and acted accordingly, even though what they were doing was conducting a war against an unarmed civilian population. The hardline attitude of the Paras and their general demeanour alienates them totally from dealing with a civilian community. They are trained in war, in weaponry and its uses. When they go into action they use only those skills. They are not policemen. They should not have been in Derry in the first place. Another regiment might have kept the march to the same area probably with no serious injury to anyone. But the central pressure on Stormont after Derry was not about the nitty-gritty details of how thirteen died and others were injured. It was yet again about the whole set-up. It was the sheer enormity of the Derry tragedy that struck terror into the hearts of the British politicians.

The simple conclusion reached after Derry was that 'something has to be done' and the British government was thinking firmly along the lines of direct rule. It could not act immediately after the Derry tragedy since that would have suggested panic, but it knew that after this things could never be the same again. Stormont was the crux. It didn't matter to Catholics that the British Army had shot its men in Derry. What was important was that it shot them because it was doing Stormont's dirty work. Even if the political decisions were being taken at Whitehall for the troops, they were in Northern Ireland to defend the civil authority, and that was Stormont. So just as everything else that had happened was pinned on Stormont's door, so too the events of Derry were seen as the work of the Unionist government. People remembered Taylor's words of July about it being necessary to shoot many more before long. They had seen internment and its violence and counter-violence. Now they saw Derry. Every single last remaining vestige of Catholic trust, confidence and reluctant support that the Stormont or Westminster governments might have had on 29 January went out the door after Derry. Prominent Catholic lawyers in Belfast, Mr James McSparran and Mr Garreth McGrath, withdrew from taking crown briefs. The few middle-class Catholics left who still identified slightly with the system decided that Derry was the limit. From 1 February the chips were well and truly down and Stormont's survival was so dubious that daily it seemed it would fold up. Faulkner's aides tried to ward off the persistent questioning.

But the feeling that Stormont was well and truly on its last legs abounded. Things just could not go on. Sometimes the feeling was hard to describe but it was easy to recognise: empty houses at parliament sittings, rapid endings to days' sittings or sometimes prolonged debates only when Paisley would raise some anti-government issue. On 4 February Faulkner went to London to see the British premier and the ministers directly involved in Northern Ireland affairs. Nothing came of the meeting, at least publicly, and Unionists, now with their backs to the wall as never before, tried to brazen out the Derry affair and put a face on their 'business as usual' attitude. But the air was heavy with gloom and already the more sane Unionists were looking elsewhere. Some even tried to get politics moving again: after weeks of dithering and playing footsy with the middle-class Alliance Party, Phelim O'Neill, a life-long Unionist and a former minister, a man who had been expelled from the Orange Order for attending a Catholic church service, resigned from the Unionist party and crossed the floor of the Commons as leader of the Alliance parliamentary party. He was followed by another former Independent Unionist, Mr R. B. McConnell, MP for Bangor, and by a Catholic MP, Tom Gormley, who hadn't attended Stormont since the Cusack–Beattie shootings in Derry the previous July, but who had also refused to attend the rival 'Catholic Parliament' at Dungiven. But the Alliance party coup of attaching support from some MPs was totally insignificant in the Stormont context. It was admittedly a unique departure and it could have had potential in a normal situation. It might have 'normalised' politics in the North but it was too late.

For by now, looking back, there was a gradual chain of events – the escalation of violence, the excesses of British troops, the Derry killings of July 1971 that had taken the Opposition out of Parliament, Faulkner's style, the internment policy, the pathetic efforts in the Green Paper and the Prime Minister's continued efforts to wring support out of the Catholic community, the thirteen Derry killings on Bloody Sunday and the perceptible decline in public confidence or trust in government and authority – and because of these events the state of Northern Ireland was, after fifty-two years, surrounded by enemies. The few friends it had wanted Stormont to dig its heels in and act more sternly, not realising that matters were completely out of control.

And now a strange turn in events was to be the very last act in the Northern Ireland tragi-comedy. The Protestant population was about to be harnessed by William Craig who was ready in early February to return to the memory of 1912 and to gather around him those Protestants who did not yet realise that their views, however strongly expressed, were making no impact on the situation at that time. On Wednesday 9 February Craig called a press conference in Belfast to announce details of his new Vanguard movement. Already for some weeks beforehand it had been an open secret that he and some of his close political friends had been meeting regularly to plan a co-ordinated campaign. As far back as October 1971, after a private meeting in Portadown, Craig had been elected chairman of a steering committee, representative of forty-three of the fifty-two Unionist constituencies in the North. A statement after that meeting pledged the new committee to 'formulate policies which will be acceptable to official Unionist constituency associations throughout the country'. And it added: 'From these policies a lead will be given in uniting the loyal people of Ulster so that their concerted voice will be listened to at Westminster, Stormont and above all at the Ulster Unionist Council.' During the months between October and February this work had not progressed very far but the loose organisation was there all along and no-one who studied the line-up of supporters which Craig had at the time was in any doubt about what the policies would be if and when they were made public. At the press conference Craig was flanked by Rev Martin Smyth, county Grand Master of the Orange Order for Belfast; Mr Billy Hull, chairman of the pro-Craig Loyalist Association of Workers (whose initials had the emotional issue of the day, LAW, tied up as if it belonged to Unionists); Captain Austin Ardill, former Unionist MP for Carrick and a bitter opponent of reform and O'Neill policies throughout the last three years; Mr George Allport, prospective Unionist candidate for Bangor; Mr Brian Smyth, representing the Young Unionists.

Allport who acted as chairman for the conference told reporters that Vanguard was not a political party but an 'association of associations'. He went on: 'I would call it an umbrella for traditional loyalist groups', and if the platform was anything to judge from, most of the groups which could so be described were indeed represented. Craig took the press conference almost single-handed apart from a long speech by Martin Smyth and offerings from other members – less articulate than Craig or Smyth – anxious to say their piece. The most important news to come from the conference was the detailed information about rallies which Craig and Vanguard proposed for various centres throughout the North. One was to be held on the following Saturday in Lisburn and more would take place at other towns and villages culminating in a final monster rally in Belfast's Ormeau Park on 18 March. As events would show, the man who picked the dates for the rallies was a superb if unwitting timer: Vanguard was to get more than its share of publicity as political events unfolded and direct rule approached.

The Lisburn rally was a quiet, orderly affair but it managed to shock television viewers and newspaper readers when reported. On a fine afternoon about 1,000 people gathered to watch and listen. What they saw struck some as amusing, others as sinister and dangerous. For, having arrived in an ancient limousine flanked by a motor-cycle escort, Craig walked along lines of men drawn up in front of the main platform.

About 500 men were marshalled in blatant military fashion and Craig moved along the ranks inspecting them, shaking hands now and then and nodding greetings to men with war medals on their breasts and bowlers on their heads. His speech was strictly vintage Craig: anti-government sentiments on the security question built around regret at the changes introduced in 1969. At the end of the rally Craig read a long and detailed Ulster Covenant reminiscent of the 1912 document which pledged the Northern Protestants to fight Home Rule for Ireland. The 1972 version was not much different except that its emphasis was directed against virtually any political initiative the British might introduce. As he finished reading the covenant Craig asked all those who assented to 'raise your hands three times and say each time "I do" '. The 1,000-

strong meeting responded and in a flash memories of the Blueshirts, the Nazis, the neo-Fascist groups of pre-war Europe sprang to mind. It was a sickening sight but it was perhaps not as sinister as Craig's own speech. Although the saluting distracted from that speech Craig made the first significant threat of recent times against the anti-Unionist population. He had begun at Lisburn in fairly low, familiar key. But at one stage he told his audience: 'We are determined, ladies and gentlemen, to preserve our British traditions and way of life. And God help those who get in our way.' The crowd cheered and clapped. The phrase was to ring through news bulletins and to read starkly in the black and white of newsprint. Some people could not believe it had been said and its author let free without even a question from the police. The big question was: what did Craig mean? That force would be used if the British touched the constitution, or only if they dumped the North into the Republic? It was depressing to hear no word of condemnation from a Unionist MP, let alone a cabinet minister. The Prime Minister and his colleagues remained totally silent. For backbench MPs in the Unionist party a sort of fool's pardon may excuse this silence: for three years these men had been in the main a hopeless and unthinking collection of yes-men who agreed to anything successive unionist governments did, no matter how unpopular or incorrect, the desire to retain the seat at Stormont overriding everything else. But on the part of government, silence in the face of Craig's speech and behaviour was criminally irresponsible. It was left in fact to Boal and Paisley to attack Craig. Boal told a local television interviewer that even to imply the use of force in the situation as it was then in March was 'very dangerous and irresponsible'. He said it should be recognised that people who are frustrated and fearful are generally a prey to the suggestion that force is the only solution. In the Northern Ireland situation, he went on, if people so encouraged were not given specific targets they would find their own targets, innocent Roman Catholics. 'And if that happens it brings this community not one step but a dozen steps closer to civil war.' Paisley joined Boal in attacking the Vanguard leader's speech and the militarism of the rallies.

But Vanguard was well underway and gaining support. If the press conference had announced it, the Lisburn rally had launched it firmly on the market. And there were plenty of buyers. In the weeks that followed there were rallies all over the North. Craig even managed two some Saturdays, arriving at one in an open car and speaking, then taking off in a private plane to swoop from the clouds to his cheering supporters at the next. Heady, emotional stuff in speech and action was the order of the day. Each week there were more and more men in the ranks for inspection and the lines Craig looked out on as he spoke were swelling. The speeches grew tougher. At Bangor on Saturday 4 March Craig called for a full return of the old Ulster Special 'C' Constabulary, originally an addition of small shopkeepers and local men to the 'A' and 'B' Specials of the twenties. The 'C' men were even more localised and unstable than either of their fellow-groups and Craig knew of course that such a memory would appeal to his shop-keeper small businessman audiences. He was getting his support principally from those sections of the Northern population into whom a fear of Republicanism and a change in their British way of life could be instilled quickest, and also from dissatisfied Unionists and ambitious young men anxious for power of any kind. Craig told the Bangor rally : 'If the government do not mobilise the people the people will mobilise themselves.'

The day after the Bangor rally, a Sunday, Craig was interviewed on RTE by Northern correspondent Liam Hourican. Craig told his interviewer that any initiative from the British which planned to put Republicans into a Stormont Cabinet – (that was the current off-the-record leak from London) – would be made impossible by Protestants. He went on to talk about a situation in which loyalists might be led to take violent action against people they considered the enemies of Ulster. 'Would this mean killing all Catholics in Belfast?' he was asked. 'It might not go so far as that,' replied Craig, 'but it could go as far as killing. It could be similar to the situation in the 1920s where Roman Catholics identified in Republican rebellion could find themselves unwelcome in their places of work and under pressure to leave their homes.'

And most people knew exactly what Craig meant: exactly as Boal had said weeks before, the targets would have to be found and they would be Catholics. The crude criterion used to determine the extent of an individual's support of the state was, once again, religion. There was still no announcement from Faulkner and it seemed reasonable to conclude that, as the rallies went on and the speeches got tougher, Faulkner at least decided to turn a blind eye to Vanguard in public and to use it privately in bargaining against the British. For the argument that Vanguard was gathering strength was now a useful piece of political ammunition for the empty Faulkner locker. He could present himself and his government to Westminster as being open to reform and forward-looking and warn against any initiative lest Craig and his wild men should spring into action. Craig had made Vanguard into the tightly-knit product of years of hard work; once dismissed by O'Neill in 1969 he had set off on the lonely and at times ludicrous trail of speaking to almost every Unionist and Orange group on the North. In three years, there cannot have been many Orange-Unionists hands that he did not shake, many Unionist associations he did not address and many members of the main Unionist party whom he did not get to know personally. As it became apparent to Protestant right-wingers that the government's policies over the years 1968-72 were 'appeasement' Craig had managed to gather around him the cream of Unionist and Orange hardliners, the best of the Northern right-wingers whose hearts yearned for the pre-1968 days of outright and unchallenged Protestant Unionist control over the Northern State. By tapping the fears of Protestant workers he won LAW to his side. The Orangemen, particularly in Belfast where Smyth who led them was a close friend of Craig's, were his too. The Apprentice Boys of Derry, still smarting after two years without their traditional parade in their city, joined Craig also, again as much out of frustration with the overall situation as from any positive enthusiasm for what Craig preached from his platforms. Thus every single Protestant organisation linked with what is euphemistically called 'traditional Unionism' was now either in Vanguard, or at least strongly represented in it.

To attack Craig and Vanguard then would have required a political courage and a reforming zeal which Faulkner quite simply did not have. In other words, while Faulkner as Prime Minister should have attacked Vanguard, he could not do so as a Unionist and leader of the party without alienating his support within the party even more nor did he have any real desire to do so: he had always liked Craig personally, especially in the final days before O'Neill sacked his Home Affairs Minister – a decision which Faulkner had opposed within the cabinet at the time. Besides Craig and Vanguard had tapped and were harnessing the support of the Protestant working-class. As has been seen, that section of the community was already frustrated with the security situation and the obvious failure of the security forces to beat the IRA. When the government spoke of hitting back at gunmen and reports continued of gun attacks in Belfast and elsewhere, there was rage that more gunmen, more IRA men, weren't being shot dead. Initially it was a problem for the security forces, but it reflected on Faulkner.

Vanguard offered some hope, if not of marching to battle at least of joining something positive. It provided Protestants who were disillusioned with the Unionist party, uncertain of Paisley and searching for a new home, with something to do. Its success was as understandable as that. Vanguard then had a logic and a base for its existence at least as representative of the people as the government. Faulkner refrained from attacking it outright by name and in his only reference to it at Killinchy in mid-February he referred to rallies as 'alien' and 'sinister' and said the determination of the Unionists not to be coerced was stronger than 'any comic opera activity can convey'. He never criticised Craig personally.

The final rally in Ormeau park on 18 March was a massive display of Protestant strength. More than 60,000 turned up, and men and women in para-military style uniforms obeyed shouted commands and stood to attention. Flags were presented and salutes taken. The platform this time included the former MP for South Antrim at Westminster, Sir Knox Cunningham, who made an enormous gaffe when he suggested to the crowd that Enoch Powell might lead the Unionist cause at Westminster. Since the most forceful issue in Powell's policy on the North had been to abolish Stormont and have full integration with the United Kingdom Sir Knox's speech was coldly received. The crowd were presumably gathered not so much to oppose Britain as to oppose any idea of union with the South. The loudest cheers came for anti-Republican sentiments and Craig's call for boycotting goods from there. Ironically, just a week before the final British moves, Vanguard was turning out to be the hastener of the initiative. The one thing the British were not sure of was the Protestant reaction. Vanguard showed them what it would be: that despite the emotion, the marching men, the para-militarism of the movement and the huge numbers, the gut-Protestant reaction would be not against any British move, but against any British move that involved the slightest hint of union with the South. For Vanguard demonstrated in public the level of enthusiasm there would be for opposing the British to keep the connection with Britain: little or none. The rallies took their style from those of 1912 which, too, were plainly not so much against the British as against what the British would do: sell out the Protestants to the Catholics in the South. Therefore by aping former glories the Vanguard movement was simply articulating, along with the frustrations of the day, the old Unionist reaction: No Surrender. And when Unionists say that they mean one thing and one thing only: no united Ireland. True, Stormont was a figurehead and the best example of living Protestant power around, but it could be dispensed with as long as the authorities did not hand over the North to Lynch and his men. So by coming out in the open Craig and his colleagues demonstrated the potential of the Protestant backlash. And it was small. Paisley wasn't there, Boal wasn't there, 'the moderate', that is to say, less hard-line Unionists weren't there. Those who were there attended more because of anger and frustration than out of any desire to fight Britain. When the British government looked at the rallies they found much to understand in the motives of those present: on security, law and order and suchlike they shared Vanguard's annoyance.

But the only logic the Vanguard message had was in its opposition to the idea of a united Ireland. True, the words were those of fighting talk, but the average man in the crowd at Ormeau Park cared little about Stormont which was to him a vague, remote concept which he had rarely if ever identified with. The men at the top in Vanguard would and could and did talk about the importance of retaining the Parliament but it meant little to their average followers whose single remaining aim at the time was quite simply to stay British. If they were sold out to Lynch by the British, then they would fight, but not unless and until that happened.

So as the crowd spilled away from the Ormeau rally its strength and its emphasis was in a strange way comfort to the British. Every element was now out in the open. They knew how everyone thought. There would be no Protestant violence, maybe some initial unrest but nothing the Army couldn't handle. Over the weekend of 18 and 19 March Edward Heath and his ministers were finalising plans for the coming week. Mr Brian Faulkner would be arriving at Downing Street on Wednesday and they had something important to tell him.

8 DIRECT RULE

As Brian Faulkner was preparing to leave Belfast on Tuesday 21 March the signs from Westminster were that Edward Heath was ready with a firm package of proposals to put to the Stormont government. The British had made up their minds; if they didn't accept them they could quit office. Faulkner was as confident as ever, firmly believing he still had the 'special relationship' with Heath, convinced that Heath was a 'friend of Northern Ireland' (that is a friend and supporter of the Unionist party) and convinced equally that, whatever initiative would be proposed it would not alter significantly the Stormont system. He was prepared for some give and take on internment but for little else.

Faulkner took to London with him his deputy, Senator J. L. M. Andrews, whose father had been John Andrews the mid-thirties Prime Minister. Andrews is the least political of all Unionists: a solid, easy-going man with a steady mind, unspectacular but safe. Faulkner could depend on him completely as a supporter. There would also be the added advantage that when Faulkner was getting excited, Andrews would keep his cool. The civil servants that went to London were the most senior: Sir Harold Black, the cabinet secretary, and Mr Kenneth Bloomfield, deputy secretary. Faulkner also took his private secretary, Mr Robert Ramsey. As the bags were packed there was an air of confidence, and, questioned about the London rumours, Faulkner's non-travelling team back at Stormont Castle smiled confidently and said nothing would change. There is no indication whatever that any of them, except the most pessimistic, foresaw any radical initiatives.

But things had very much changed in London and the eventual decisions were reached only at the end of a discernible train of events, every one of them as easily visible to Faulkner in Belfast as to the British in London. Faulkner had drawn one set of conclusions, the Heath government a different set. What had happened in the British cabinet over the year may be summarised as follows.

When Faulkner came to office, the mixture of panic over Chichester-Clark's resignation and awe at Faulkner's ability, had gained the Stormont Premier some early support among cabinet ministers, Heath included. It seems clear, however, that at no time did there exist between Heath and Faulkner anything like a 'special relationship' or a special understanding as was suggested in Belfast. Heath is generally agreed to have a style of premiership which allows his ministers to get on with their own jobs. He takes them into his confidence when he needs to, but otherwise they get on with their own work. Faulkner, he treated much the same as he would another junior minister: as long as the Stormont Premier was doing the job and not being too awkward he would have a free hand. No incident upset this situation until the Derry killings in July 1971 and the Opposition walk-out. Even then Faulkner was able to convince Heath that by October the truants would be back with their tails between their legs and normal politics would be resumed. For six months or so, until the decision to intern, Heath had no cause to turn his personal attention to Northern Ireland. As Faulkner was getting on with the job, Reginald Maudling, the Home Secretary, was reporting 'all well', or at least that things were not getting worse.

With internment, the greater involvement of British troops, the appalling publicity that resulted from the operation, the disastrous and underestimated reaction among the Catholic population, Heath began to think again about Faulkner. The single thing that most worried him was the failure of the Stormont government to estimate the reaction. When Faulkner sat down at the cabinet table in August to plead the internment case, he hadn't made a point of telling his British masters that the policy would completely shut the door on Catholic co-operation, alienate them totally from both Stormont and British governments and escalate violence to such an extent that in one calendar year more would die violently than at any period in Irish history for fifty years. Heath had accepted that the policy would create problems. But he trusted Faulkner's own assessment of their size. And that assessment was disastrously wrong.

Soon after internment an inner cabinet in Britain, consisting of Heath, Maudling, the Secretary of State for Defence, Lord Carrington, and the Lord President of the Council and Leader of the Commons, William Whitelaw, with occasional help from the Foreign Secretary, Alec Douglas-Home, began to turn attention to Northern Ireland. The government at Westminster had Common Market problems and problems on the industrial front, but Carrington particularly had warned against forgetting Northern Ireland and was in favour of a transfer of security powers in early September, soon after the first internment orders were signed.

By the end of October, many Tory minds were made up on Northern Ireland : there would have to be firm, decisive action, it would have to be dramatic and radical, it would have to be direct rule. The party held its annual conference about then and it was from there that the Downey story in the *Irish Times* had come. Two weeks later there came Paisley's revelations about direct rule and then the 'initiative' trail had begun. So it is clear that from very soon after internment the British government had been thinking along fairly radical lines. The decision not to take any action then was as much due to Maudling's caution within the inner cabinet as to any willingness to try and let the Stormont government itself settle the matter. Maudling was continually counselling against the need for any action at all, Carrington favoured the transfer of security (although not necessarily for a softer line :

indeed many London observers believe he favoured such action so that the British could move more swiftly against gunmen and the IRA generally) and there are indications that Whitelaw had all but made up his mind that sooner or later he would be on the way to Belfast himself to act as Secretary of State. Indeed in January 1972 a story circulated to this effect and was never denied.

The British decided that no action could be taken until after Christmas. In January, even before the events of Sunday 30th in Derry, the inner cabinet had revealed details of its thinking on the crisis to the whole government which received the news with something approaching horror, certainly with great surprise. The whole Irish question was clearly in the melting pot. It had been indeed since the speech by Harold Wilson, the leader of the Opposition, in the previous September. He had received a guarded welcome for his ideas, particularly on internment and the transfer of security, even from the Tory party. So that by the following January there had been major progress within the Conservative party, and more vitally, within the Conservative government on the Irish question.

Maudling, the advocate of 'wait and see' was shattered by the Derry killings and told his colleagues that time was on no-one's side. The last obstacle in the way of a move was gone with his change of mind and heart. Faulkner came to London on 4 February and although little if anything leaked from that meeting with Heath it seems clear that in a guarded, subtle way the British ministers put out many feelers to indicate the way they were thinking. They got no response at all from Faulkner. To every suggestion Heath made, for example for a move on internment, Faulkner produced an answer or an objection. The British realised they would get nowhere by coaxing, nowhere by negotiation.

That was February. The delay in moving after that seems to be attributable to the working out of the precise details. But one important event occurred which served

133

both to slow up the move towards direct rule and to make even more clear the way the British government was thinking.

In the last week of February the High Court in Belfast gave a vital ruling in a case involving John Hume, Ivan Cooper and others. The two MPs had been arrested in September in Derry and charged, and found guilty of, not obeying the orders of a British soldier. The group appealed and the case eventually found its way to the High Court where, in a reserved judgement the Lord Chief Justice, Sir Robert Lowry, and Mr Justice Gibson and Mr Justice O'Donnell upheld the appeal of Mr Charles Hill and Mr James McSparran on behalf of Hume, Cooper and their colleagues. The case was complicated but basically the appeal had been that the Northern Ireland government had, by regulation under the Civil Authorities (Special Powers) Act providing that British troops could arrest under that Act, acted *ultra vires* the government of Ireland Act 1920 which specifically reserved to the Westminster parliament the power to make laws for the Army and armed forces. It was a technical point, but the Belfast High Court upheld the appeal and a legal – and political – victory was won against the administration.

The Westminster parliament then had to pass, rapidly, an Act indemnifying its Army for all its activities in Northern Ireland and it was during the course of debate on this legislation, The Northern Ireland Act 1972, that some revealing statements were made in the House of Commons and in the Lords. The first came from the Home Secretary, Maudling, speaking in the Commons and replying to MPs who had raised wider questions about the transfer of security.

He said: 'I know there are considerable feelings one way or another about the transfer of responsibility for law and order. This is a very big issue indeed which must be discussed and can only be discussed in the broad context of a total settlement for Northern Ireland. By passing this Bill tonight we will do nothing to prejudice the argument on that one way or another.' There it was, and from the Home Secretary himself . . . 'the broad context of a total settlement for Northern Ireland'. And there was more.

When the Bill went to the Lords very little notice was taken of it because the late-night sitting made sure that their Lordships' speeches were scantily covered in the press. Hansard proved interesting reading. At one stage the Lord Chancellor, Lord Hailsham had this to say: 'I said before and I repeat that I thought events will probably overtake this measure in various ways some of which I can foresee and some of which I am not sure that I can foresee.' Later he said: 'I think probably events will overtake this Bill which is less important than some people have thought.'

Maudling's and Hailsham's statements coincided almost exactly with the final decision taken by the full British government to move towards direct rule, by moving to take over full control of security powers in Northern Ireland. If anyone in Stormont noticed these statements in the Commons and Lords either they chose to ignore them or they kept their fears to themselves.

When Faulkner and his party arrived at 10 Downing Street shortly before 11.30 a.m. on the morning of Wednesday 22 March, they smiled and waved for photographers before disappearing inside to begin what had been forecast by government sources at Stormont as 'about four or five hours of talks'. Flanked by Andrews, Faulkner was quickly facing Heath, Maudling, Carrington and Whitelaw, then Lord President of the Council, Leader of the Westminster Commons and close confidant and friend of Heath. The GOC Northern Ireland, Tuzo, was also present and he gave an up-to-date assessment of the security situation. His report was routine, none of the Stormont delegation sensed anything strange or unusual about it and even if it was unhopeful for the future, what could one expect in the circumstances. Then Heath chipped in on the internment issue and Faulkner agreed that there should be some move on the release of men, as quickly as was safe and with the advice of the security forces. Still nothing seemed out of the ordinary and Faulkner talked enthusiastically about the success rate against the IRA and the theory that the structure of both Official and Provisional wings was being badly hit. Heath, who is said to lapse at times into long silences, hold his head up and gaze into the distance, came out of one such pose and in a few sentences gave Faulkner the fright of his political life. He told him bluntly what the British, not proposed, but decided to do. No options, no discussion, the mind was made up.

The British had not only decided to take over complete control of security matters, including the Royal Ulster Constabulary, the RUC Reserve and all executive responsiblity for law and order, but they had also decided to take control of the courts, responsibility for the administration of the law and justice including the organisation of and appointments to the bench, all matters of public order, prisons and penal establishments, all special powers, public prosecuting and power to create new laws and penal offences. In other words, they had decided to take every single worthwhile power in the security and legal fields away from Stormont. A moment's thought was enough for the Stormont delegation; they would be left with absolutely nothing to govern. With so many ministries in Belfast staying in business only to rubber-stamp measures from Westminster, with local authorities already stripped of power in the fields of housing and development and with what Heath now proposed to do, a Stormont 'government' would have literally nothing to do except in the development field where even then British money would be required to finance anything at all of major proportions. It was unthinkable. Faulkner could literally not believe his ears. As Heath spoke and the clock ticked on towards lunch-time the Stormont delegation began to ask whether their stewardship had been bad, what they had done wrong, where they had failed to live up to their promises. But lunch-time intervened. An hour or two to think things over.

Executioners and condemned men, by all accounts, had hearty meals and the lunch lingered for more than two hours. Back at the table Heath and his colleagues took up where they had left off before lunch and the precise details of the plan were outlined to Faulkner. At about 4 p.m. ministerial cars were drawn up to the front door of No. 10 but after a few minutes they backed away again and it was announced that 'a false alarm' had caused the movement of vehicles. What had happened was that door-keepers had seen Faulkner and Andrews leave the Cabinet room and, presuming this meant the meeting was over, had summoned the official cars. But what occurred was the first major break in the discussions. It happened when Faulkner could literally take no more of what he was hearing and asked for a break to talk things over with his colleagues. The meeting broke up, Whitelaw went down to the House of Commons for a short time and 'half-time' (for the second time round) was taken in the negotiations. During the break the Stormont delegation contacted their counterparts at Whitehall and their absent colleagues at Stormont. In the Stormont Commons, shortly after 5 o'clock, news that the meeting was still going on was received anxiously by Ministers and MPs. None of them knew very much about what was happening, but the longer the meeting went on, they reckoned, the worse it was for them and their chances of survival. In the end the meeting lasted more than 9 hours, twice as long as the expected time. Faulkner and his colleagues did their best to smile as, surrounded by pressmen, they made their way from the door of 10 Downing Street to waiting cars.

As Faulkner's car sped away it was all over for Stormont. Of that no-one had any doubt. The meeting had been a disaster for Stormont. Nothing Faulkner had said had made the least impact on Heath and the only reason now that an announcement was being delayed was to allow Faulkner tell his cabinet colleagues. He told Heath that they would resign, that they could not stomach a security transfer and continue in office. 'Tell them anyway,' said Heath, 'and see what they say.'

The Stormont delegation went home late that Wednesday night and the next morning a full cabinet meeting took place in Stormont Castle. Faulkner gave the details of the previous day's meeting with Heath. It would be the understatement of the year to say he took most of his colleagues by surprise. From Roy Bradford, Minister for Development, there was a muted, muttered 'I told you so', for indeed Bradford had regularly warned that Stormont would be closed down by the British. No-one paid any more attention to him than they paid to the many newspaper leaks, many of them now proving to have been accurate. After meeting his ministers, Faulkner telephoned Heath as arranged the night before. He told him that the Northern Ireland cabinet had considered the British government proposals for a complete transfer of security powers to Westminster and that, as he had forecast, his colleagues to a man found the terms made them unable to continue as a government. Heath expressed his thanks for the not unexpected news and told his own colleagues at once that Faulkner and Andrews would come back later that day. This time, there would only be discussion on how the plan would be executed. The negotiations were really over.

Later on Thursday, Faulkner and Andrews went back to Downing Street where the Stormont Premier agreed that he and his colleagues would stay at their desks until the necessary legislation was through both houses of Westminster. He and his colleagues heard that Whitelaw would be Ulster's Secretary of State and they learned of a plan to set up an advisory commission to assist the new secretary. They were given as many of the details as they could take. This second meeting lasted only a few hours. It ended with the customary false smiles and handshakes for television cameras and photographers on the doorstep. If there was anyone, anywhere in the world whom Faulkner would have wished not to smile and shake hands with it was Edward Heath. The man he thought he could depend upon to allow the Unionists to continue uninterrupted in office had let him down, humiliated him, taken his powers, his government, even his parliament, away from him. And with the implications of the decision still ringing through his head, Faulkner took himself home to Northern Ireland shortly after midnight on Friday morning. Heath would make an announcement at 11 o'clock in the morning. It would say, in more words than were necessary, 'Direct Rule'. Faulkner and Northern Ireland would have no difficulty in understanding what it meant. The show was over and all that was to come now was the shouting, and one final fling by Faulkner to try to justify to his supporters – and indeed opponents – his political career as Prime Minister.

Very late on the Thursday night a long statement from Stormont Castle set out in detail the proposals which Faulkner and his government had made to the British in the days after the terrible events of Derry's 'Bloody Sunday'. That day was 30 January, and on 4 February, Faulkner had gone to see Heath for a 'routine visit'. At that meeting the two Prime Ministers agreed that 'at a suitable time' an initiative should be taken. Faulkner went back to Belfast and genuinely began to work on some form of political initiative. He still had not realised that events in the North, since his arrival in office, since internment, since Derry's fatal Sunday, were moving far too swiftly for any politicking. Anyway, he and his cabinet applied their minds to modifications of and additions to the Green Paper of October. It was still the basis but, as the late night statement showed there were some interesting modifications which Faulkner would have been well-advised to have released to the public. At a meeting of the Unionist Party Standing committee in Belfast on 4 March, he did hint at some of them but no-one paid much attention since Faulkner speaking straight was difficult enough to grasp but Faulkner dropping hints was almost impossible to pin down: an interpretation put on his words in good faith would be denied by him if it did not accord with his own views on the topic in question.

Among the proposals which he made to Heath, by

letter on 1 March, was a unique one for a rejuvenated Council of Ireland.

The Thursday night statement said:

'We suggested a far-reaching effort to secure a constitutional "new deal" in Ireland as a whole, under which Northern Ireland's right to self-determination would be recognised by Treaty, there would be a common policy and action for the suppression of illegal organisations, including the concept of a "common law enforcement area" in Ireland making the return of fugitive offenders automatic, and a joint Irish Inter-Governmental Council would be set up with equal membership from the Belfast and Dublin Governments, to discuss matters of mutual interest, particularly in the economic and social spheres.'

Such ideas while not daringly radical at least suggested that, even if it was another effort to save Stormont, Faulkner was trying to see things in an all-Ireland perspective. His 4 March speech for example had been remarkable for its absence of Faulkner-style blood-curdling references to the IRA, to the Republic as a foreign and alien state and other such warlike sentiments. On the idea of a referendum for the North's population on the border issue, Faulkner had suggested a first vote whenever forty per cent of the members of the Stormont Commons asked for it. 'We proposed that a change in the constitutional position should require a majority of those entitled to vote and that there should be an interval of not less than five years between referenda unless at the previous referendum more than fifty per cent of those actually voting had voted for change.' Again, not a very radical policy, but a thought at least on the referendum issue, one of the issues, incidentally, leaked by British government aides to English reporters before Faulkner had talked to Heath about it.

What really riled Faulkner was that he didn't even get a reply to this letter of early March, there was equally no response to his speech to Unionists a few days later. At that time, with his undoubted gift for news management, he might have benefited by letting more of his people know how he was thinking. Certainly had he released to the world his ideas on a Council of Ireland he would seriously have embarrassed Mr Lynch in Dublin and probably caught his London masters on the hop. But he kept the cards close to his chest, depending – as it was to prove falsely – on his 'friendship' with Heath to win through.

So as Heath rose in the Westminster Commons that Friday morning a long fifty years of tension and turmoil, and quite literally of blood, sweat and tears was coming to an end. So was a horrible nightmare of three years during which the death-toll of innocent and not-so-innocent men, women and children, had mounted steadily. The figure was more than 300 for just thirty months of violence as the British government eventually moved with a dramatic initiative. British soldiers had died, policemen, Ulster Defence Regiment members and, most tragically of all, completely innocent Protestant and Catholic people caught in the terrible spiral of a guerilla war being fought out in cities and towns.

Stormont came to an end through a combination of elements some of which it could have controlled with more careful tactics on the ground earlier, most of which it could have avoided through more generous attitudes years beforehand. As the strings were pulled together and began to fall into the hands of Edward Heath and his British colleagues they made an ugly pattern indeed: fifty years of Unionist and Protestant rule had forced to the top all the bitterness and tension inherent in any one-party state and made worse in the Irish situation where the twin pyres of religion and politics fired each other. The simple and mild civil rights demands of the late sixties had been met grudgingly and found wanting very quickly. The terrible sectarian rioting of a week in August had set alight once more the flames of religious hatred in Northern Ireland. And from Belfast to Derry, Newry to Ballymena, religious hatred is but the shorthand for the struggle between Unionism and the various forms of Republicanism, whether violent or constitutional.

By the time Brian Faulkner was on his way to the last famous London meetings with Heath just in March, nothing he could do, nothing that could happen and nothing anyone could think of would make the least difference to the decision to end uninterrupted Unionist rule in Northern Ireland. It will be a political surprise perhaps even surpassing its death, if the body of Unionist control ever rises again anywhere in Ireland.

APPENDIX

The last sitting of the Stormont House of Commons took place on Tuesday 28 March 1972 at Parliament Buildings. Papers, orders under various acts, were presented purely formally and the outgoing Prime Minister, Mr Faulkner told the MPs assembled for the last time in the huge chamber that Royal Assent had been given to a number of Bills. The Speaker, Major Ivan Neill, Unionist MP for Ballynafeigh read letters of resignation from two Democratic Unionist MPs, Mr John McQuade who had been MP for Woodvale and Mr Desmond Boal, outgoing member for Shankill. Both men were resigning because, they said, they could not remain members of a non-functioning assembly. Boal's letter was particularly caustic about the direct rule move:

Dear Mr Speaker,

The people of Northern Ireland have been substantially deprived of their democratic right to participate in the making of laws for their own governance, and that too for an indefinite time, if one reads the proposed legislation in another place. For the moment I am not concerned with the fact that this seems a poor reward for a people which has endured for some years the combined assaults of bombers and propagandists, nor with the fact that the persistent obtuseness of the Unionist administration has contributed to its own demise; nor even with my belief that the proposed arrangement will succeed only in angering one section of the community and eventually disappointing another while depriving both of a salutary and even therapeutic means of expressing such feelings.

My purpose is rather to convey to you that I have no intention of concealing from the people who elected me that I am no longer, except in the most legalistic sense, their representative. I will take part in no charade, no matter how

143

elaborate, at the whim of an insensitive and clumsy Westminster. Having therefore no desire to remain a member of a parliament that does not exist, I tender you my resignation from the seat for the division of Shankill.

Yours faithfully,
Desmond Boal.

McQuade's letter was more straightforward:

Dear Mr Speaker,

I am not prepared to be a public representative without powers, nor have I any wish to remain a member of a parliament that does not function. An example has already been given to the country of members who have been prepared to draw their salaries for a representation they refused to perform. I am not going to follow that example. The people who elected me are being deprived by the will of Westminster of their right to be represented. I do not propose to hide this from them. Nor do I hide the bitterness and sense of betrayal that both they and I feel at the treatment meted out to us by the British Government. Whatever service I may perform in the future will not be as a powerless member of a nominal parliament. I therefore tender you my resignation from the seat for the division of Woodvale.

Yours faithfully,
John McQuade.

For Boal, resignation was as much a gesture of contempt for Stormont as for Westminster. It would mean little if any change to his life. For McQuade the sacrifice was great: a docker by livelihood until he had got the Woodvale seat in 1965, he now proposed to return to an unsteady life and an unsteady income, leaving the security of a Parliamentary salary of more than £2,000 per annum. The two men's gestures have not so far been followed by any other Unionists.

Faulkner made a brief statement on the adjournment debate and was followed by Reverend William Beattie (South Antrim), Captain Robert Mitchell (North Armagh),

Mr Vivian Simpson (Oldpark), Mr Roy Bradford, the Minister of Development, Mr Bertie McConnell (Bangor), Mrs Anne Dickson (Carrick), Mr James Strong (Mid Armagh), Sir Robert Porter (Lagan Valley), Mr John Laird (St Anne's), Mr Joshua Cardwell (Pottinger) and Mr Herbert Whitten (Central Armagh). The adjournment was then moved by the Deputy Speaker and Chairman of Ways and Means, Mr Walter Scott (Bloomfield) and after Mr Beattie called for a division the House passed the motion to adjourn by 20 votes to 4. Apart from Mr Beattie, Mrs Dickson, Mr Laird and Mr Stronge registered protest votes against the new arrangements by voting against the motion.

There followed expressions of thanks by and to the Speaker and, as Hansard reported the House: 'Adjourned accordingly at fifteen minutes past five o'clock until Tuesday April 18th, 1972 pursuant to the Resolution of the House of this day'.

The adjournment to 18 April was of course technical since before the Commons could reassemble again it would be prorogued for one year. Not all MPs were present for the final sitting, apart from the Opposition who were quietly celebrating their political victory elsewhere, some Unionists were absent.

Paisley was absent too and his absence has lost the occasion some of its history. The following is a list of the MPs and Senators entitled to have been present on the last day at Stormont. They are in alphabetical order with their constituency and party, as well as any office either in government or of the House which they held at the time of prorogation. All were elected at the General Election of 1969 except where otherwise stated. This does not apply to the Senate which has a more complicated system of election. Since the 1969 election two MPs resigned (not counting Boal and McQuade on the last day): they were Lord O'Neill of the Maine (Bann Side) who left parliament shortly after receiving his title when he resigned as Prime Minister and Mr Richard Ferguson (South Antrim) who resigned in late 1969 for health and pressure of work reasons. One MP, Dr Norman Laird (St Anne's) died during the life of the parliament and was succeeded in the seat by his son John. One Senator, John Barnhill was murdered in December 1971 after he had tried to foil an Official IRA attempt to burn down his Co. Derry home. His attackers opened fire and shot him in the head.

THE COMMONS

Anderson, Albert Wesley (Derry City, Official Unionist). Parliamentary Secretary Minister of Home Affairs

Babington, Robert John (North Down, Official Unionist)

Bailie, Robin John (Newtownabbey, Official Unionist). Minister of Commerce

Beattie, Reverend William (South Antrim, Democratic Unionist Party). Elected to Commons April 1970 in by-election

Boal, Desmond Norman (Shankill, Democratic Unionist Party). (Resigned on day of final sitting, would have been entitled to sit in House until letter of resignation was read)

Bradford, Roy (Victoria, Official Unionist). Minister of Development

Brooke, Captain John (Lisnaskea, Official Unionist). Chief Whip and Deputy Leader of Commons

Burns, Joseph (North Derry, Official Unionist). Parliamentary Secretary, Ministry of Health and Social Services

Caldwell, Thomas (Willowfield, Independent)

Cardwell, Joshua (Pottinger, Official Unionist)

Carron, John (South Fermanagh, Nationalist)

Chichester-Clark, Baron the Lord Moyola of Castledawson, James (South Derry, Official Unionist, former Premier)

Cooper, Ivan (Mid-Derry, Social, Democratic and Labour Party, withdrew from Parliament July 1971)

Craig, William (Larne, Official Unionist. Lost Party Whip in Commons early 1970, crossed floor to face government in October 1971. Technically an 'official' Unionist but he voted against government law and order policies)

Currie, Austin (East Tyrone, SDLP, withdrew from Stormont July 1971)

Devlin, Paddy (Falls, SDLP, withdrew from Stormont July 1971)

Dickson, Mrs Anne (Carrick, Official Unionist. She resigned the Party Whip in the Commons in March 1971 but took it back again about a month before direct rule)

Dobson, John (West Down, Official Unionist. Former Leader of the House)

Faulkner, Brian (East Down, Prime Minister and leader of the Unionist Parliamentary Party from March 1971)

Fitt, Gerry (Dock, Leader of the SDLP. Withdrew from Parliament July 1971)

Fitzsimmons, William (Duncairn, Official Unionist). Minister of Health and Social Services

Fyffe, William Samuel (North Tyrone, Official Unionist)

Gormley, Thomas (Mid Tyrone. Independent until July 1971 when he left parliament along with other Opposition MPs. Gormley refused to take part in the Assembly of the Northern Irish People, the Opposition's parliament and in February he joined the Alliance Party becoming one of their first Parliamentary members)

Hall-Thompson, Major Lloyd (Clifton, Official Unionist)

Hume, John (Foyle, SDLP. Withdrew from parliament July 1971. Was President of Opposition Assembly)

Kelly, Basil (Mid Down, Official Unionist). Attorney General

Kennedy, John William (Cromac, Official Unionist)

Kennedy, Patrick (Central, Republican Labour. Withdrew from parliament July 1971 but did so independently of other Opposition MPs although for same reasons. Only surviving member at Stormont of Republican Labour Party formerly led by Fitt)

Keogh, Michael (South Down, Nationalist. Withdrew from parliament July 1971)

Kirk, Herbert (Windsor, Official Unionist). Minister of Finance

Laird, John (St Anne's, Official Unionist)

Long, William (Ards, Official Unionist). Minister of Education

McConnell, Robert (Bangor, Independent until February 1972 when he became a member of the Alliance Party and one of their three MPs at Stormont)

MacIvor, Basil (Larkfield, Official Unionist). Minister of Community Relations

McQuade, John (Woodvale, formerly Official Unionist. He lost the Party Whip in early 1970, later became a member of the Democratic Unionist Party. Resigned his seat on 28 March, when parliament met for the last time)

Magowan, Samuel (Iveagh, Official Unionist). Assistant Chief Whip

Minford, Nat (Antrim, Official Unionist). Leader of the House of Commons

Mitchell, Captain Robert (North Armagh, Official Unionist)

Neill, Ivan (Ballynafeigh, Official Unionist). Speaker of the House of Commons

O'Connor, Roderick (West Tyrone, Nationalist Party Leader in parliament. Withdrew from parliament July 1971)

O'Hanlon, Paddy (South Armagh, SDLP. Withdrew from parliament July 1971)

O'Neill, Phelim (North Antrim. Formerly an Official Unionist, he joined the Alliance Party in February 1972)

O'Reilly, James (Mourne, Nationalist. Withdrew from parliament in July 1971)

Paisley, Reverend Ian (Bann Side. Elected in by-election April 1970, he was leader of the Protestant Unionist Party until in late autumn of 1971 he formed with Boal, Beattie and McQuade, the Democratic Unionist Party. Only a week before direct rule Paisley had been elected Chairman of the Public Accounts Committee of the Commons)

Porter, Sir Robert (Lagan Valley, Official Unionist)
Scott, Walter (Bloomfield, Official Unionist). Deputy
    Speaker of the House of Commons
Simpson, Vivian (Oldpark, Northern Ireland Labour Party)
Simpson, Dr Robert (Mid Antrim, Official Unionist)
Stronge, James (Mid Armagh, Official Unionist)
Taylor, John (South Tyrone, Official Unionist). Minister
    of State, Ministry of Home Affairs
West, Harry (Enniskillen, Official Unionist). Minister of
    Agriculture
Whitten, Herbert (Central Armagh, Official Unionist)

THE SENATE

Cairns, Joseph (Ex-Officio by virtue of being Lord Mayor
    of Belfast)
Andrews, J. L. O. (Official Unionist). Deputy Premier
Barnhill, John (Official Unionist). Killed by gunmen in
    December 1971
Cameron, Millar (Official Unionist)
Cunningham, Lt. Colonel J. G. (Official Unionist)
Drennan, John (Official Unionist)
Elder, Nelson (Official Unionist)
Gibson, Dunlop (Official Unionist)
Glentoran, Rt. Hon Colonel (Official Unionist). Speaker
    of the Senate
Johnston, John Stewart (Official Unionist)
Kennedy, Norman (Labour Party)
Kinghan, Samuel (Official Unionist)
Lennon, Gerard (Nationalist. Withdrew from Stormont
    parliament July 1971. Became 'speaker' of the Alter-
    native Assembly)
McClelland, David (Official Unionist)
McClure, Ina (Official Unionist)
McCullough, Charles (Formerly Official Unionist he joined
    the Democratic Unionist Party when it was formed)
McGill, Dr P. F. (Nationalist. One of the few Opposition
    politicians to remain in parliament after July 1971)
McGladdery, Daniel (Official Unionist). Parliamentary
    Secretary in Premier's Office

Mallon, Patrick (Nationalist. Withdrew from parliament July 1971)

O'Hare, Patrick (Nationalist. Withdrew from parliament July 1971)

Stewart, William (Official Unionist)

Taggart, Mrs Edith (Official Unionist)

Wilson, Patrick (SDLP, withdrew from parliament July 1971)

Wilson, Major William (Official Unionist)

Wilton, Claude (SDLP, withdrew from parliament July 1971)

No person apart from those listed above was entitled to be present at the final sittings of Commons and Senate. Dr G. B. Newe was a member of the cabinet and government at the time of direct rule but only by virtue of a special use of a provision of the Government of Ireland Act 1920 which allowed him, as it had allowed Mr David Bleakley before him, to hold office for a period of not more than six months. Newe was not however entitled to sit or speak in either House.

When the house adjourned for the last time in both the Commons and Senate, members queued up to take parting farewells with the respective Speakers. In both Houses final Order Papers were signed as souvenirs.